HENRY FORD

Roger Burlingame was born in New York City and studied at Harvard University. After a brief career as a journalist and war correspondent, and several years in book publishing, he turned to writing full time. He is best known for *The American Conscience* and for his several biographies and books about American technology and mass production, including *March of the Iron Men* and *Engines of Democracy*. Mr. Burlingame died in 1967.

Henry Ford

BY

Roger Burlingame

Quadrangle/The New York Times Book Co.

THIRD PRINTING, March 1976

HENRY FORD. Copyright © 1954 by Roger Burlingame. This
book was first published in 1955 by Alfred A. Knopf, Inc.,
New York, and is here reprinted by arrangement.

First QUADRANGLE PAPERBACK edition published 1970 by
Quadrangle/The New York Times Book Co., 10 East 53
Street, New York, New York 10022. Manufactured in the
United States of America.

International Standard Book Number: 0-8129-6123-4

ACKNOWLEDGMENTS

I am greatly indebted to Mr. A. K. Mills, Director of Archives, Mr. Henry Edmunds, Archivist, and his assistants Messrs. Owen Bombard and Stanley Graham of the Ford Motor Company for generous assistance throughout the preparation of this book. On a visit to Dearborn I was abundantly provided with accurate factual material. No information that I requested was withheld, no questions were asked as to what use I might make of it; my complete freedom was respected, and I encountered fewer formalities than is usual in research libraries and manuscript collections.

I wish to renew my thanks to the staffs of the Yale University Library, the New York Public Library, and the Engineering Societies Library, the members of which have assisted so many of my past researches. I appreciate the interest and assistance of Elmo Roper, who generously offered to read my manuscript and made several valuable suggestions, and I acknowledge help also from my old friend Kenneth Littauer.

I

"I DON'T know anything about history," Henry Ford once said to an interviewer,[1] "and I wouldn't give a nickel for all the history in the world. The only history that is worth while is the history we make day by day. Those fellows over there in Europe knew all about history; they knew all about how wars are started; and yet they went and plunged Europe into the biggest war that ever was. And by the same old mistakes, too. Besides, history is being rewritten every year from a new point of view; so how can anybody claim to know the truth about history?"

That was 1916, and since the world war had begun, and especially since the grimly ludicrous failure of his mission to get the boys out of the trenches by Christmas 1915, Ford had been an increasingly bitter pacifist. His repeated attacks against "militarists" and munitions-makers, his pronouncement that nations and flags were "silly," his refusal to take part, or encourage his employees to participate, in the "preparedness" drive infuriated patriots in those days when the American war spirit was already smoldering. In June, when attention was diverted from Europe by incidents on the Mexican Border, President Wilson ordered the National Guard to patrol duty and the

[1] John Reed, the brilliant young writer later involved in the Russian revolution.

people were stirred to an outburst of flag-waving and band-playing; but Ford, it was reported, threatened militiamen in his employ with loss of their jobs if they obeyed the President's call. Without checking, the *Chicago Tribune*, whose patriotism has always been unpredictable, emitted an editorial scream to the effect that Ford was an ignorant idealist and an anarchist. Ford denied the report and brought suit for libel against the *Tribune* for a million dollars.

It was nearly three years before the suit came to trial. The trial opened three years, almost to the day, from Ford's first estimate of history. In those years old stories had been rewritten in Europe; molds of politics, morals, and technics had been shattered. Ford himself had gone into reverse, thrown his plant open to war work, and even offered to rebate his war profits to the government. In the histories most Americans had written for themselves, the United States had won the war, and in their crystal balls they saw eternal peace. The millennium was here—provided only that we kept clear of European entanglements. The people—the common people of the vast midlands, which in 1919 were still the world's breadbasket— they and Henry Ford had come half-circle to meet each other. On the rough seats of their Model T's they all rode together into the dawn of a new prosperity.

That was how our world was when eight lawyers representing "the world's greatest newspaper" walked into the red brick courthouse in Mount Clemens, Michigan, intent on making a monkey of the world's greatest industrialist. Ford faced them with a counsel of his own consisting of seven of the state's most brilliant attorneys. As far as can be gathered from the records, none of them seems to have done him a particle of good. Day after day, it is said, they drilled him behind closed doors—coaching, cramming, as a tutor crams a late boy for his exam—but the man whose company's profits at that moment were reaching a rate of sixty million dollars a year did not listen. Or, if he heard, he forgot. Or, perhaps, it seemed, as he sat there, swinging his long, bony leg—"a slight boyish figure," as Reed had said, "with thin, long, sure hands, incessantly moving . . . the fine skin of his thin face browned by the sun: the mouth and nose of a simple-minded saint; brilliant, candid, green eyes"—it seemed, perhaps, that he did not care.

He could remember the revolutions per minute of his flywheels. But the *Tribune's* lawyer, Elliott Stevenson, did not ask him that. He asked about the Revolution of 1776, and the witness was vague. Ford could not place Benedict Arnold or explain the fundamental principles of American government. It was an easy trick for the defense counsel. The muffed answers to the schoolboy questions brought plenty of laughter in the packed courtroom. Yet few of the spectators or the farmer jurors were ever quite convinced that the *Tribune's* lawyer had really scored. Ford's own attorneys were desperate at the thought of their hard training gone glimmering, but there were times when the audience wondered if the cross-examiner had not been left holding the bag. Once they were sure of it. "What," asked Stevenson, "was the United States originally?" Ford unclasped a jackknife and began to sharpen it on the leather of his shoe. Then, without looking up, he answered: "Land, I guess."

The defense was reported to have spent nearly half a million dollars on its preparation. "Ignorant" is a broad term, and counsel drove to extremes to justify it. Ford was asked to read something aloud to the court and it seemed that he went along with his opponent's lawyer in the effort to prove illiteracy. No; he had forgotten his glasses. But he did, counsel asked, sometimes read? Seldom, Ford replied, except the headlines.

"Mr. Ford," Stevenson persisted, "I have some hesitation but I think in justice to yourself I shall ask this question: I think the impression has been created by your failure to read some of the things that have been presented to you, that you could not read. Do you want to leave it that way?"

"Yes," the witness answered, "you can leave it that way. I am not a fast reader and I have the hay fever and I would make a botch of it."

To the newspaper's lawyers this must have seemed like a final triumph, but with the rustic jury and out along the dirt roads the answer won new affection for the man who was changing the American geography. Friendly laughter swept the prairies like a west wind;

farmers, spelling out the words in the papers by lamp-light, slapped their thighs and called their wives to listen; they shouted to one another above the loud explosions as they cranked their little cars that "Hen-ery," like themselves, was too busy to read!

"History," Ford was on record as saying, "is more or less bunk. It is tradition. We want to live in the present, and the only history that is worth a tinker's dam is the history we make today."

So in the weeks before the verdict the press of the nation had a field day. Editorials, quips, and cartoons ran the gamut from comic ridicule to humorless con-tempt. In one session of the trial the interviews of 1916 were paraded, and those papers that had been too busy for it then now took up the hound cry: So history is bunk! There is no doubt that many Ameri-cans who had sweated through the American school system at least as far as the eighth grade privately nodded agreement, and in ten hours of deliberation the jury could not bring itself to the admission that the producer of more than two million automobiles, who had reduced the retail price to less than five hundred dollars, was an ignoramus even if he was illiterate. Nor did it seem logical that one who was well on the way to becoming the nation's richest citizen should be an anarchist either. On the other hand, the jury-men could not believe that their peer had suffered fi-nancially from the *Tribune's* editorial. Their verdict, therefore, was for Ford with six cents damages.

For more than ten years Ford had reversed the

prophecies of the sharpest guessers in the high eche-
lons of finance. He had upset the orthodox free-enter-
prise pattern and scrapped the most sacred articles of
the American business creed. He had taken the money
which might have gone in dividends to his stockholders and used it to expand his already gigantic
shop. Because the Supreme Court of Michigan had
backed the stockholders, he had forced them by an
almost unsurpassed performance of sleight of hand to
sell out to him, and he was content that they should
make 350,000 per cent on their investment because
it left him undisputable dictator. He had railed like a
Marxian communist against the "demons" of Wall
Street. Like an Owenite socialist, he had talked of
sharing profits with his workers. He had deserted the
ranks of his fellow industrialists in their opposition to
labor by doubling, at one fell swoop, the minimum
wage in his own plant.

As if this had not been enough, Ford had ignored
the dogma that "it pays to advertise." Apart from
some early announcements such as the biblical herald-
ing of the Model T—"I will build a car for the multitude"—he had been content to let the "multitude" do
his advertising for him. They had done this in an odd
manner. Humor was not a notable feature of the advertising "art" in 1919, especially if it "kidded" (or,
as current slang put it, "joshed") the product. Yet the
celebrated Ford jokes sold "Lizzie"—or so Henry
believed. In any case, they formed a body of genuine
American folklore. They were the purest Yankee dis-

tillations, as indigenous as the fables of Johnny Apple-
seed. Now, to the great flivver-driving public, "History is bunk" was just another Ford joke—true, wasn't
it, like the one that said the Model T's passengers
were its shock-absorbers?

This time, however, the principal was not amused.
In the Wayne County courthouse, giving the twangy,
hayseed answers that had brought sympathetic smiles
from the gallery, he had appeared indifferent enough.
Yet his casual air was no index to his feeling. The
grilling had burned into his soul as nothing else had
ever done or could ever do. Afterward his fear of
courtrooms was pure panic. It is one thing to smile
sympathetically when another is accused of ignorance.
It is something else to feel the dunce cap on one's own
head before the amused eyes of the world.

At about this time, however, an unease was notice-
able among historians. In 1920 the spirited English
writer, Herbert George Wells, appeared with a volume that enhanced this doubt. It was a history of
the world, no less, and it was so entertaining that it
shocked the academies. For a nonfiction book in that
twilight of a romantic era, its sale was unprecedented.
Professors who had grubbed their way over vast fields
of footnotes through all of their careers began to wake
up, look about them, and wonder if they too might
make history readable at the expense of its dignity and
pick up a few thousand dollars in the process. In
general, then, the writing of history underwent a

change. In the United States, in particular, came a growing conviction that America had a culture of its own, and this was exploited. Everywhere, also, there was revived interest in archæology; the new historians, checking written history with artifacts, found that much of the record had been slanted. Professor James T. Shotwell came to the conclusion that more truth can be learned about the period of pre-history from the study of textiles, pottery, and graves than about the literate eras from writers intent on magnifying men and events. In other words, was not history "as she was wrote" in the academic tradition more or less—well—under suspicion?

Ford could never have explained why he had said or thought what he had. Perhaps the word *history* had thrown him back to the Springwells schoolhouse, which had held him in hours when he itched to tinker with an engine. More likely it had suggested the thing that most nearly drove him berserk and resulted in the firing of dozens of his employees—the citing of precedent as proof that something could not be done. The hot rebellion in his quoted speech about "tradition" hints that he confused history with the inflexible obsessions of method that distinguish the plodder from the creator. (You can't do that! Why? Because it has never been done.) History, in short, delineates the possible, defines the impossible. Have all revolutionaries, perhaps, believed in their hearts that history was bunk?

No one knows what, during the five years or so

following the libel suit, went on in the extra-curricular thought of this true revolutionary. It has been said that he consciously determined to prove what he had meant. Possibly, as the word *history* repeated itself in his mind, he was persuaded to inquire what it truly was. It is not likely that he knew of the historians' change of mood, of the growing American cultural self-consciousness, or of the effect of new discoveries in archæology. The fact remains that a kind of history presently engaged countless hours of Henry Ford's attention and that a considerable segment of opinion had become ready to accept that kind.

Precisely halfway between Boston and Worcester at South Sudbury, Massachusetts, an "ancient hostelry" had, since colonial times, refreshed travelers on the old Post Road. It was called the Red Horse until Longfellow celebrated it in *Tales of a Wayside Inn* and from his poems it took its new name. These narratives in verse, the most famous of which is "The Landlord's Tale: Paul Revere's Ride," were written in 1863, the year of Henry Ford's birth. Whether this coincidence or the discovery of a relic of the past that was obviously not "bunk" or perhaps merely the charm of the battered old building was responsible, Ford fell in love with the Wayside Inn in 1922 and bought it the following year.

He restored it, not for himself, but for the people. He went to elaborate pains to find out its original condition and took men from the Ford plant to work at it. He opened the sixteen sealed fireplaces. He traced some of the inn's old furniture and accessories that had been sold, and bought them back. He fired one of his workers because he cut away part of a staircase, making a slight change in the original structure. The man explained that, unless the change was made, hundreds of tourists would bump their heads and sue the owner, and, after a time in which his anger cooled, Ford hired the worker back. But this was only one of many occasions that showed that the despiser of history had become a meticulous researcher and restorer of the past. It became a passion with Henry Ford to find how the people had lived—ordinary people—and to show his findings to ordinary people today.

His mind moved in strange ways, once he discovered this new direction. In the mood in which he contemplated the restored tavern at Sudbury, he went into reverse against the world he had himself created. The need to go the whole way in any enterprise he had begun led his uninstructed mind—as immune to logic and philosophy as it had been to history—into queer performances. Not content with restoring the Wayside Inn, he must restore the entire surroundings. He bought land all round it, plowed the land with old wooden plows, sowed it in grain, ground the grain in a pre-revolutionary mill, set up blacksmith shops—all to demonstrate ways of life in a world that was peculiarly remote to this most advanced practitioner of mass production.

Finally, strangest of all, he was disturbed by the sound and sight of automobiles on the Post Road running through his colonial dream! So he asked the Commonwealth of Massachusetts to detour the ancient highway. His proposal was accepted providing Ford would assume the entire expense. It cost him a quarter of a million dollars to preserve the purity of his own brand of history against the corrupting effect of thousands of his own Model T's!

The fascination of exploring the past through artifacts is, in itself, a powerful thing. To a man like Ford, whose book education scarcely went beyond McGuffey's *Readers*, it is likely that a kind of history *that needed no written words* was acutely appealing. And we know that this appeal has caught millions of "average," car-driving Americans, who agreed with Henry Ford that history was more or less bunk as long as it was held between the covers of a book. The fact, however, that Ford's pursuit of archæology was so unorthodox, so haphazard, so whimsical, and sometimes in such downright contradiction of revealed truths has led observers to seek an oblique psychological or psychopathic motive.

The restoration of the Sudbury inn was followed by a personal enterprise that occupied much of Ford's attention—and that of many of his employees—for more than twenty years. At Dearborn, to which his company had moved when Highland Park became too small, he built an immense museum. He packed

it with miscellaneous relics. His aim was to display
the entire world sequences in agriculture, transportation, communication, and manufacture from the most
primitive tools to the most advanced machines. Obviously, even in the hands of experts such a project,
if attainable at all, must develop gradually over a
long span of time, such as that in which the great
Deutsches Museum in Munich matured.

Ford was handicapped at once by his almost super-
stitious fear of experts. He always professed to believe
that experts were primarily conscious of the limita-
tions of the field in which they worked and were
therefore forever discarding as impossibilities things
that the hopeful, untutored experimenter would try.
In his industry, of course, Ford could not keep to
this prejudice, as it took the greatest mass-production
experts in the world to design the assembly-line pattern: yet even these people had to pretend, in the
boss's presence, that they were really trial-and-error
men. In the historical collections and structures, then,
he preferred to detach his own men from their shop
duties for the work, rather than to hire professional
museum curators who could have brought order into
the chaos at Dearborn. To these detached workers
he said: "Get everything you can find! I want at least
one of every tool, utensil, or machine ever used." So
the museum became Gargantuan and incoherent—a
treasure house of incalculable value if arrangement
should ever become possible—yet still the presenta-
tion of a new kind of history to the millions of school

children who, tired of their books, come every summer to look and wonder.

Around the museum Ford built "Greenfield Village," a combination of private nostalgia and a consciousness of world development. To it he brought,
intact, the house in which he was born, jewelry shops
where he had once fixed watches, the shop in which
he built his first car, and the Menlo Park laboratory
of his god, Thomas Edison. But he also brought a
seventeenth-century stone cottage from England, a
steamboat from the Suwanee River, the house in
which he erroneously supposed the song-writer
Stephen Foster to have been born, an early American glass works, a Cape Cod windmill, and other
buildings. These things were discovered by Henry
and Edsel Ford in person, brought stone by stone,
brick by brick, and put up anew in Dearborn, and
it did not occur to Henry that the planting of them
in an alien environment might seem incongruous.

Nearly all the relics have one thing in common:
they are things used by run-of-the-mill humanity, not
by potentates or any elite. Other archæological mu-
seums might parade symbols from tombs in the Egyp-
tian Valley of the Kings. Such things were not for
Greenfield Village. Ford's concern, indeed, his obsession, was the common man. The whole extravagant display, then, is supremely American: in its
vastness, its democracy, and above all in its naïve, in-
articulate, and disordered reaching into a past that the
books have ignored.

Perhaps truer than most of Ford's biographers' speculations about the intricacies of his motives were the simple reminiscences of one of the men who worked on the Wayside Inn and Greenfield Village projects.

When Mr. Ford said, "History is bunk," I do not think he meant the history of the people. When he talked of history, he thought of war and rulers. But he was very enthusiastic about bringing to the attention of the present generation the development of the past, in mechanics, different little trades, how men made barrels, how men made horseshoes. . . . It was history but not the history we get in textbooks where somebody cuts off somebody's head. . . .

All this activity by which Henry Ford sought, perhaps, to extricate himself with honor from the "ignoramus" stigma stretched into the twilight of his life. It was not a major phase. Most of it came long after his great creative years. In some ways, however, a glance at this aftermath gives more clues to the man's basic qualities than the contemplation of any other period. In the dynamic days many of Ford's doings were confused with those of his associates. His fierce obsession led him into byways of which his enemies have made much capital. It was in the aging years, however, that the roots of that obsession were exposed; never, we may think, did it become more poignantly visible than in that naïve, blundering, misdirected but intense search for a history that was not bunk.

II

JULY 1863 brought the turning point of the Civil War. The Battle of Gettysburg reached its end on the fourth. Vicksburg surrendered on the same day and the whole of the Mississippi Valley passed into Union control.

By this time, however, the final factor that determined the war's outcome had taken formidable shape. This was the tremendous industrial development in the North. Not only had the "American system" of interchangeable parts made rapid quantity production possible in hundreds of Yankee factories, but machinery had been applied to western grain through harvesters and threshers. This march toward wealth and welfare, from which the South was barred, made Northern triumph inevitable. At the same time, the war was the greatest possible stimulant to Yankee industry. The urgent need for Army uniforms and shoes brought quick development of the sewing machine; the manufacture of this and of firearms sped the march toward mass production. Everywhere, west as well as east, machine shops had sprung up and high-pressure steam engines were finding many new uses.

It is this background, and not the transient scene of war, that we remember as we note the birth of a first son to William and Mary Ford on Springwells

Township Farm near Dearborn on the thirtieth of July. The city of Detroit, which has long since engulfed this Wayne County farmland, was fast growing with new industrial enterprises. William Ford, a pioneer Scotch-Irish farmer who had come to Michigan ten years after it became a state, distrusted urban things and kept his eyes on the land. He was glad when the boy came because farmers in the West needed boys.

William Ford was successful; his farm paid; but Mary Litogot's inheritance may have been a factor in his prosperity. Her ancestors seem to have been Dutch: thrifty, hard-working, with a talent for the soil. Like most pioneer farms, the Fords' was largely self-sufficient, having its own sawmill and gristmill and machinery for making homespun of wool sheared from Ford sheep. As the boy grew, only the machines attracted him.

Nothing William Ford could do would turn Henry's attention to crops or stock. He loathed plowing and planting, feeding and milking. He ran away from the jobs that were his natural lot as a farmer's boy—the chores that were as much the daily portion of a Michigan country lad as the milk he drank—and he would be found where some wheel turned or red iron glowed on an anvil. Henry was useful in these places. He found broken plows, harrows, mowers, and reapers and mended them: he kept the saws sharp in the sawmill. But he was never what William Ford meant when he said a farmer needed boys.

He went to the primitive Springwells school and led the other boys away from their jobs to watch him build water wheels and steam turbines. He learned nothing in school except epigrams from miscellaneous literary classics that were quoted in McGuffey's *Readers*. He never learned to spell, to write a formed hand, to read freely, or to express himself in the simplest written sentence. But from the earliest time of which there is any record he was a master of mechanical logic: from a glance at any machine he could understand the interdependence of its parts—follow a line of reasoning, however long, through gears, ratchets, spurs, cams, and levers.

It was usual for this boy, once he had put the home tools in order, to mount one of the farm horses and ride, bareback and barefoot, to the farms of neighbors and fix their things. He did this for fun—or to escape the smell of the cows—and he would take no money. At twelve he developed a passion for timepieces. He seems to have ridden over much of the country, picking up clocks and watches that needed repair, taking them home, working on them into the late night, and returning them better than new. If Henry had taken fees for this work, his father might have forgiven him. But his refusal either to help the farm pay or to establish himself in an earning trade led William Ford to doubt his son's mental balance. The pressure of these doubts must have scared Henry, for along about his fourteenth year he began to work secretly at night at his bedroom workbench.

Like all times of which no written note is ever made, these years must be only vaguely remembered. Henry himself told about them forty-odd years later and his amanuensis wrote it down. Other boys and girls of the Dearborn region also had memories and, in the effort to show what made this strange giant tick, a story got pieced together that probably is mainly true.

Henry must have been about twelve when, along the road that ran from the Ford farm to the Plymouth carding mill, he saw a belching locomotive. He had seen locomotives on rails pulling trains, but never on a country road. He had also seen steam engines like this used to run threshing machines or sawmills, but always they were hauled to the farms by horses.

He was sitting, at the time, in a farm wagon full of wool for the carding mill. Without speaking, he got down off the seat and followed the engine, which was moving no faster than a man could walk. His father called to him; perhaps Henry did not hear. The cacophony of the steam monster must have been loud as he came up behind the engineer's platform, but the sound, the sharp smell of the smoke, the red sparks falling on the road, and the white plumes of steam shooting from the cylinders—these were music and drama that the voice of William Ford could not interrupt.

Without preamble, the boy began asking questions of the engineer. They were technical questions about horsepower and revolutions per minute. The engineer could hardly believe the words that came in the treble voice. How did a boy know enough to ask such things? Henry Ford could not tell him.

Henry did not write down the engineer's answers or what he learned from watching steam at work. It was never his habit to write things down. He fitted details into a logical train of thought. Reasoning from one point to the next in a mechanical sequence, he could always find the item he needed. He learned to do this so fast that it was said he was "intuitive."

The vision of the road engine did not leave him. While he worked at his watches—repairing some three hundred and building one complete from scratch—the monster was there in the back of his mind, moving without horses or oxen and bringing to the farms the power that could do away with the drudgery and perhaps make farming a congenial oc-cupation. It came in between his other thoughts, which were many and often highly ambitious but al-ways geared to machines.

At sixteen, he could stand the farm no longer. Arguments with his father contributed to his discom-fort. He went to Detroit and got an apprenticeship in a machine shop that made steam engines. As he was only paid $2.50 a week and room and board cost him $3.50, he worked at night for fifty cents a night repairing clocks and watches in a jewelry shop. Thus he combined his two main interests.

It is said that the jeweler he worked for—a former Dearborn neighbor named Magill—concealed Henry in the back of the shop lest customers seeing so young a lad doing repair work lose confidence and take their precious timepieces away. Henry, however, enjoyed the work so much that he forgot to be humiliated by his experience. The delicate work presented him with a fine contrast to the heavy materials of his daytime job. For a time he seems to have been tempted toward a career of watchmaking, and the comment on this in his autobiography is illuminating:

I thought I could build a serviceable watch for around thirty cents and nearly started in the business. But I did not because I figured out that watches were not universal necessities, and therefore people generally would not buy them. . . . Even then I wanted to make something in quantity.

Here is the first evidence of the obsession that dominated Ford's life. Already his interest was in the plain man who would have no use for luxuries. Watches, in those days, were still luxuries—at least in Michigan, though several Yankee manufacturers had begun their quantity machine production in the East. It had not yet appeared possible to Henry that a luxury could be turned into a necessity by the cheapening process of large-scale manufacture. Soon after this, however, he was diverted forever from watches.

He was able to complete his apprenticeship in the engine shop and qualify as a machinist long before his time was up. His first real job took him back to the vision on the Dearborn road. It was with the local representative of the Westinghouse Company as an expert in the setting up and repair of road engines. From then on the dream of a vehicle moving under its own power was never for a moment interrupted.

The dream was, of course, by no means unique with Henry Ford. Steam carriages had run successfully and even commercially on English roads for some fifty years. Various kinds of steam vehicles had been tried in France, Germany, Austria, and the United States. In 1879, when Ford was sixteen, George Baldwin Selden, of Rochester, designed a gasoline-motored car and applied for his celebrated patent.

Because his training had been with steam, Ford thought first of a steam vehicle; because he had grown up on a farm, his first efforts were in the direction of a light tractor that would pull a plow. He actually built such a machine with a kerosene-heated boiler, and this taught him an important lesson. He soon saw that a high-pressure boiler light enough for such a vehicle was dangerous.

For two years [he tells us] I kept experimenting with various sorts of boilers . . . and then I definitely abandoned the whole idea of running a road vehicle by steam. I knew . . . there was no difficulty in designing a big tractor for use on a large farm. And . . . the manufacturing of a big tractor which only a few wealthy farmers could buy did not seem to me worth while.

Here again, the obsession prevailed. Nothing for a small, expensive market would ever be worth while. So Ford began to think that perhaps, after all, the farmer would be "more interested in something that would travel on the road than in something that would do the work on the farms" and began to study the internal-combustion engine, which needed no boiler and no water tank, and which derived its power directly from the explosions of its vaporized fuel. All over the world experiments were being made in the design and construction of such engines, so he was hardly sailing on uncharted seas.

In the meantime a curious thing had happened. Henry had gone back to the farm. His reasons, as he explained them later, were characteristic. They were not precisely those of a prodigal son. We can find no impulse of repentance or hope of winning his father's forgiveness. He went back entirely to advance his chosen non-agricultural vocation and to increase his contentment with that career.

He tells us that his father offered him forty acres of timberland, provided he gave up being a machinist. In the same paragraph he explains that, having accepted this condition, he was able, as soon as he moved back, to build himself a first-class machinist's workshop! He then set up a sawmill with a portable engine, cut his trees into lumber, and, because he was anxious to get married, built a house for himself and his bride. There is no record of his ever doing any farming, except for some occasional machine-threshing, and "when I was not cutting timber, I was working on the gas engines." His father's disappointment is hardly surprising, but he learned in those years that

nothing in the world would ever be allowed to inter-
fere with this son's ambitions even if Henry had to
resort to subterfuge to gain his ends. It was at about
this time that the farmer neighbors to whom the soil
was sacred said that the young man had "wheels in
his head" and his father remarked to a friend, speaking of his other sons:

"John and William are all right but Henry worries
me. He doesn't seem to settle down and I don't know
what will become of him."

There are fragmentary stories about Henry's
courtship of Clara Bryant of Greenfield Township;
of his driving her in the winter in a sleigh he built
himself. An elderly Dearborn neighbor still remembers their husking bees when the discovery of a red
ear gave the privilege of a kiss. Young Ford must
have been appealing in his early twenties, slender,
handsome, with the straight, sensitive features that
reflected many generations of the best American stock
and the abundant mustache, according with the custom of the time, which he abandoned before the
custom was over. And the neighbor remembers too
that "Hank," as they called him, was "a nuisance talking about his gas-buggy."

Henry and Clara were married in the spring of
'88. It is probable that no genius of such cantankerous
ways and unpredictable moods ever had a more devoted wife. For nearly sixty years she gave him constant attention, cheer, and courage as well (as her

Episcopal Litany says) in all time of tribulation as in the time of prosperity.

With the coming of the 1890's there began a frenzy of experiment with what in Europe was called the "motor car" or "automobile"; in America, the "horseless carriage." These designations indicated the difference in concept which dominated the design of self-propelled vehicles for some fifteen years. Americans, deeply conditioned by the tradition of the horse as motive power, spent time, money, and effort vainly trying to make steam, gas, or electric motors propel buggies, victorias, surreys, and runabouts over the deeply rutted and muddied roads of their continent; whereas Europeans, having well-built, hard, smooth roads to start with, invented something quite new to run on them—something from which all thought of the horse had been eliminated. No doubt the bicycle, which could be used everywhere on French and German roads, had helped the catharsis in the minds of automobile inventors there and purged them of the memory of animal traction. Thus by 1894 the French Levassor, assisted by the patents of the German Daimler had produced a car that in its essentials differs little from today's standard automobile. In the United States, however, at this time, the few vehicles that—given perfect road and weather conditions—were able to boast their horselessness were combinations of mechanical features nearly every one of which had to be abandoned.

It seems curious in these days of instantaneous international communications that technology could have advanced in such opposite directions in Europe and America little more than fifty years ago. Yet even in the United States men were experimenting in various places without knowing what one another did. Hiram Maxim, intensely concentrating in 1892 on putting a gasoline engine into a tricycle, writes in his memoirs:

I was blissfully ignorant that Benz and Daimler in Germany; De Dion, Panhard, and a host of others in France; Napier and a few others in England; Duryea Brothers, Haynes, Apperson Brothers, Winton and others in the United States—were working might and main on gasoline-propelled vehicles. . . . As I look back, I am amazed that so many of us began work at the same time, and without the slightest notion that others were working on the same problem.

Henry Ford, however, knew about the buggy built and driven by the Duryea brothers in 1892— said to be the first gasoline-motor vehicle in America —at Springfield, Massachusetts. He knew it because, slow as he might be in reading, he read every newspaper or magazine article he could find on the subject that occupied every instant of his spare time. He was, at the moment, an engineer at the Edison Illuminating Company—later the Detroit Edison Company.

He had left the farm for good in 1891. Becoming increasingly restless there, he had spent more and more time in Detroit. One day he had met an old acquaintance who had worked with him some eight years before when he had been an apprentice in a machine shop. This man, John Wilde, had since gone into the Edison company, and he offered Henry a job there. Henry had reported for work the next morning and had won quick approval by immediately repairing an engine stoppage that had baffled everyone.

He had advanced rapidly until he held the job of chief engineer. But, though he was conscientious and effective, he knew that the work was not his life job. At best it was a useful potboiler. His heart was in a woodshed behind his rented home on Bagley Avenue. There, at night, he worked with what tools he could afford on a project of his own. A new stimulus came with the news of the Duryeas' triumph.

Ford's project was a tiny vehicle that would be driven by a two-cylinder four-cycle motor. Concerning the engine his machine-shop studies and experiments with models gave him confidence. But on the design of the car, the building of its frame, its wheels, its transmission and differential, he was working in the dark. The experiments he read about were all different. The Duryeas and Charles B. King, an accomplished engineer who was extremely helpful at this time, both used wooden carriage wheels. The Duryea buggy, built for a horse, had large wheels in the rear and smaller ones in front, while King's were the same diameter front and rear. Elwood Haynes startled

Washington in 1894 with a small affair mounted on bicycle wheels. All these mechanics struggled blindly through trial and error with clutches, countershafts, belts, sprockets and chains, and steering devices.

Ford's mechanical difficulties, however, were nothing compared with the low level of the morale factor. Experiment with "horseless carriages" made a man a social outcast. An elderly Detroiter remembers that Henry was known in his neighborhood as "Crazy Ford." During this time his wife seems to have kept up his courage as, night after night and all night on Saturday, he worked, tried, failed, tried again with crude tools and makeshift materials while the neighbors watched the little brick shed with its late light as if it contained a sinister maniac. Perhaps that painting done in Norman Rockwell's most romantic mood of Clara crocheting while Henry tinkers is truer than it looks.

In 1895, however, there came a boost to Ford's morale the consequences of which lasted all of his life. He had become chief engineer at the Edison power plant. He was invited to a banquet and conference with the great inventor himself. In the course of the evening, after Edison had made an address about the future of electricity, Ford managed to get his ear—something of an achievement, no doubt, in view of Edison's deafness.

I told him [Ford remembers] what I was working on. . . .

And then I asked him if he thought there was a future

for the internal combustion engine. He answered something in this fashion:

"Yes, there is a big future for any light-weight engine that can develop a high horsepower and is self-contained. . . . Keep on with your engine. If you can get what you are after, I can see a great future."

From that moment the "Wizard of Menlo Park" became Ford's idol. It has been said that Edison was the only god Henry ever worshipped with full humility.

The little job in the shed was finished on a spring night in 1896. It would not go out the door; Ford, in his impatience, picked up an ax and knocked down part of the wall. Then, at four in the morning, in the rain, he ran his first car round the block. This was the trial run. Later, after a few alterations, he took Clara and the baby Edsel for a drive before astonished crowds. He drove it often after that, followed by the laughter of running boys and the curses of drivers of frightened horses. Whenever he left his strange toy on the street a dozen people tried to run it, so that he had to chain and lock it to lampposts.

The "car" was mounted on bicycle wheels—a considerable advance over the buggy wheels of the Duryeas, but one in which Ford had been preceded by Elwood Haynes—and its transmission consisted of a belt from the motor to the rear wheels. There was no reverse gear.

One reason for the advance attained by the bicycle wheels was a psychological one. If there was any way to divert the mind of the observer from the horse that was not there, it was desirable to use it. The wire-spoked, pneumatic-tired wheels recalled something that was extremely popular at the moment—something with which the horse had nothing to do. The bicycle was, indeed, a first escape from the horse, and, as such, it is entitled to the credit that several writers have given it of being "the father of the automobile." In any case, such wheels had been almost universally adopted for light cars by the turn of the century.

Ford built two other cars before, in 1899, the Detroit Edison Company delivered its ultimatum that he must either give up his job or his hobby. By this time, however, Detroit had taken him seriously. The tremendous excitement that in four years had swept the country had been stimulated by widely, sensationally publicized races and shows in the big cities. A magazine, *Horseless Age*, had acquired large circulation, and speed and endurance tests were crowding other events off the sports pages of the newspapers. Manufacturing companies had been founded with aggregate capital of nearly four hundred thousand dollars. As Detroit did not want to be left trailing this whirlwind, its prouder citizens hailed the pioneers King and Ford.

When Henry, therefore, quite naturally chose to abandon dynamos for motor cars, several capitalists were willing to help him—or be helped by him. A company, called the Detroit Automobile Company, was formed to exploit a car Ford was then designing. Altercations with his backers forced Ford's resignation before the car was finished, and a new corporation called the Henry Ford Automobile Company came into being. Within a year there was new controversy, and it began to look as if this strange, stubborn, brilliant pioneer was going to be exceedingly difficult to get along with.

There are two stories about what happened in these years from 1899 to 1902. One states that Ford had become bewitched by an impulse of speed and had wasted his time and the money of his financiers designing and building racing cars instead of producing a salable product. The other—and this is Ford's —is that he was wholly dedicated at the time to the concept of a low-priced car and that this idea had no other supporters.

The whole thought [says Ford in his autobiography] was to make to order and to get the largest price possible for each car. And . . . I found that the new company was not a vehicle for realizing my ideas. . . . I resigned, determined never again to put myself under orders.

It is possible that both stories are true. We know that Henry was, at this time, determined to enter track races as a means of publicity. He hated racing for itself. He did not believe that capacity for high speed added to the value of a car. But he knew that, at that particular moment in automotive history, break-

ing records at track races was the way to celebrity, and
thus to the kind of backing that would give him real
power.

If he had been given such power in these first companies and been allowed to build a low-priced utility
car instead of a "rich man's toy," he might never have
built a racer. Being thwarted in this dominant ambi-
tion of his life, however, he simply made use of the
company's funds to attain fame and authority for himself. This, at any rate, is the probability; for it is almost
certain that the obsession of large quantity and low
price was already there.

There was no doubt about the fame. The first
great triumph came in 1901 when he won a track
race in fashionable Grosse Pointe, Michigan, with a
car of his design. In another event he reached the incredible speed of seventy miles an hour. Finally, a
fabulous monster called the "999," built with the
collaboration of Tom Cooper, broke all records—
again at Grosse Pointe—over a three-mile course
with the daredevil Barney Oldfield driving. This time
the news went round the world, and it was an ignoramus indeed who did not recognize the name of Henry
Ford.

The location of the main events is important. Everywhere, at that time—in Europe as in America—
the automobile was a perquisite of the rich. Imported
cars had been bought by sporting millionaires in New-
port and New York. But even the American "horseless carriages," being handmade, were expensive, and

the idea of a car being useful was thought absurd. The steam and gasoline buggies were operated by people who were accustomed to drive pairs of "spanking" horses in light runabouts or "traps."

As long as motor cars remained in this category Ford had no interest in them. He despised rich men and all their works. A luxury that gave airs to the wealthy and served no utilitarian purpose was anathema to him. Not only was he dedicated to the needs and desires of "plain folk" like himself—people with simple tastes and small incomes—but, obviously, these millionaires' playthings could never be produced in quantity and Ford was already addicted to the mass-production concept. Nevertheless, if he was to get the financial support he needed, he must first capture the imagination of the wealthy. And, most certainly, Grosse Pointe was the place to do it.

A month after the 999's victory the rich man appeared in the person of Alex Y. Malcomson, a Detroit coal dealer who was present at most important sporting events and who, after watching Oldfield come within inches of destruction at better than a hundred miles an hour, was convinced that the best investment for future profit was in the automotive industry. Malcomson sought out Ford and made the first approaches to the deal that ended in changing the face of America.

III

NONE who was there ever forgot the meeting in the office of Malcomson's coal company on the evening of June 15, 1903. Several had reason to remember with bitterness the doubts and misgivings that followed it. Yet, in the sweep of the revolution that in the first two decades of the twentieth century carried the United States to such peaks of prosperity and industrial power, it was hard to think back to the uncertainties of 1903. It was exceedingly difficult to remember that in the visible portents of that year there was little to indicate the coming tastes and temper of the American people. One reason for this difficulty is that much of the power to direct that temper and nurture those tastes lay in the hollow of one man's hand. He was present at the meeting in the coal dealer's office, one of the less impressive figures in a group of prominent businessmen, and still unaware—as they were—of his potential.

Fear, distrust, or derision of the motor vehicle was still a dominant impulse among run-of-the-bank Americans. Let the millionaires play with this dangerous show-off thing and keep it to themselves in places where it need not terrify the horses of hardworking farmers! The only good automobiles ever did these country people came when they broke down or were ditched in the deep mud and a farmer brought his honest Dobbins to the rescue for the highest consideration he dared demand. Such folk could hardly be expected to master the complexities of the new machine when even the wealthy with all their special education had to hire foreign servants called chauffeurs to drive it.

One hardy adventurer had, indeed, tried to break the prejudice. Ransom Eli Olds, after experimenting with steam, had moved from Lansing to Detroit and, impelled by the heretic motive of producing a simple car for the "masses," was turning out little one-cylinder, curved-dashboard runabouts at the rate of four thousand a year and selling them for $650 "including mudguards." The apparently growing popularity of this small two-seated gasoline carriage was the only sign that interest could be awakened outside rich and sporting circles. It also showed that quantity production and low price were possibilities. Yet the bulk of the sales was in cities; these sales had been stimulated by a great deal of remarkably clever advertising, and it was suspected that the gay little Oldsmobile might be meeting a passing craze for a vehicle obviously designed for pleasure rather than utility.

Thought about all these things had been moving through the minds of the men who gathered on the fifteenth of June to take the plunge with Malcomson. Some of them had backed and filled, hesitated, said yes and then no and then yes again; in the end it was Malcomson who had convinced them. "Malcomson is a success," lawyer John Anderson wrote to his father, "in all kinds of business," and the conservative banker John Gray offered his cash wholly because of his confidence in Malcomson. James Couzens and Charles Woodall were Malcomson's employees and reflected his enthusiasm. Anderson and Horace Rackham were Malcomson's attorneys. The Dodge brothers had agreed to come along because they could not lose—Malcomson had arranged that. None of these men had agreed to the deal solely because of confidence in Henry Ford. They all knew about Ford and about the 999. But it was to Malcomson that they gave their money—because Malcomson believed in Ford.

Some of them did not give any money. Malcomson preferred other contributions. To assemble his product he would need some sort of factory building: He knew of a suitable place owned by a German woodworker named Albert Strelow. He induced Strelow to turn over his shop in exchange for company stock. He gave stock to John and Horace Dodge, who made motors and transmissions for Olds, in exchange for a contract to make these things for his new company instead. Ford was to pay for his stock in expert services. He had designed the car the company would build.

All these matters and several other details had been arranged before the meeting. Labor, wages, cost of materials, price to be charged, had all been calculated.

In this plant [Anderson wrote in the letter to his father] there will be ten or twelve men at $1.50 a day

together with a foreman. They will assemble the car,
paint and test it. You can see how small the manufacturing expense will be.

We figure to sell for $750 without a tonneau and
$850 with a tonneau. We figure our costs for the job
without tonneau will be $554 and $50 more with the
tonneau. . . .

It is amazing the way the thing has been started.
Everything has been done since last October.

Everything had been done, in other words, since
the day Alex Malcomson had seen the 999 come in
half a mile ahead of all competitors on the Grosse
Pointe track. The meeting on the fifteenth of June
was a formality. It was held merely as a preparation
for the swearing in of the incorporators—to make
sure there was full agreement. The articles of incorpo-
ration specified a stock issue with par value of $100,-
000. The meeting agreed to the stock distribution.
The control—fifty-one per cent—was divided between Malcomson and Ford.

On the morning of June 16 the incorporators were
sworn in and the Ford Motor Company was a legal
fact. More than two thirds of the capital was in the
form of shop, machinery, patents, contracts, and
promises. After a great deal of scurrying about, borrowing, and making drafts on savings, a total of $28,-
000 cash was raised. On this shoestring Henry Ford's
dream hung; during his lifetime this initial outlay was
never augmented by a penny from any outside source.

During the summer of 1903 Ford, vice-president,

Couzens, secretary and business manager, and the Dodge brothers were the only ones who were actually engaged in making cars. The Dodges made most of the parts of the car in their separate shop, gambling heavily in future sales of the completed automobiles to pay for materials and labor. As Allan Nevins has recorded:

This machinery—engines, frames, transmissions, axles —was brought from the Monroe Street [Dodge] machine shop on horse-drawn hayracks. Each running gear was dumped on a given spot on the [Ford] factory floor and given careful inspection and testing. If it was satisfactory, other parts were brought up for assembly.

Ford's small working force dealt with four cars in a group; when they were finished, the group moved on to another four cars. Two or three men usually worked on each car.

This primitive method of assembly is interesting to review. By 1903 tremendous strides had already been made in the progress of the "interchangeable parts" system of manufacture toward mass production in other products. Sewing machines, bicycles, firearms, and agricultural machinery were manufactured on a pattern of minute division of labor and a methodical arrangement of machine tools so that each worker in a Colt or Singer plant, for example, performed only a small operation. But the automobile in 1903 was in an early experimental stage: no detail of engine or transmission was settled, no design of any part frozen; there was no standardization of tools or processes, and

it was not until four years later that true interchangeability of parts even among supposedly identical cars
made in a single factory was demonstrated by the
Cadillac Automobile Company. In 1903 there were
more than twenty-five American manufacturers of
passenger cars and, with the exception of Olds, no
manufacturer sold more than a few hundred cars each
year. The automobile, therefore, was for the most part
a strictly handmade article.

Ford's first dream crystallized in a gay, brightly
colored little affair not unlike the Oldsmobile in design. It was called "Model A" or, somewhat imita-
tively, the "Fordmobile." Its eight-horsepower engine
under the seat had two opposed cylinders. Its planetary transmission gave two speeds forward and one reverse. The crank was at the side. The twenty-eight-
inch wheels had wooden spokes. A steering wheel
replaced the tiller. The complete car weighed eleven
hundred pounds. It was found necessary to advance
the price slightly above the estimate. It was advertised
"as a runabout" for $800; the detachable tonneau was
$100 extra.

It was a tough summer for the little shoestring
corporation. More than six hundred of the little cars
were assembled; after sales began, reports came in
that Model A refused to climb hills. Ford rigged an
incline running up to his second story and ran his cars
up it, day after day, to test them. He wanted to halt
shipments until the trouble was found; Couzens told
him this would mean sure bankruptcy, so Ford in-

stead sent mechanics to help the complaining customers until the fault was corrected at the factory. The
difference in the points of view of the two men is revealing both of their characters and of the tension of
the times. Ford, already something of a perfectionist,
did not want to send out an imperfect car; Couzens,
the businessman, knew that only quick sales could
save the company's finances. The Dodges had delivered the parts; they were deeply committed for
materials; by their contract they were entitled to take
over the sales of the Ford cars if their obligations were
not met, and this would have meant the end of the
company. Finally, as the year moved on, it was seen
to be the turning point of the industry; the demand
was growing daily, and under the heat of the competition any delay would be fatal. On the other hand, the
appearance of a Ford missionary mechanic in the hills
of Pittsburgh or San Francisco was quickly appeasing
to a disappointed purchaser.

When that hurdle was jumped, however, another,
still more threatening, loomed ahead. This stemmed
from an event that was celebrated in its time and
probably had a farther-reaching effect on the early
American automobile industry than any other. This
was the organization of the A.L.A.M.—an association based on a legal fiction—which managed to hold
a kind of sword of Damocles over Henry Ford's
head for eight years.

The Association of Licensed Automobile Manufacturers was formed by a group of companies that

had been alarmed into paying royalties on a patent granted to the supposed inventor of the gasoline automobile. George Baldwin Selden, a clever patent attorney who played with internal combustion engines on the side, had built such an engine in 1877; two years later he had drawn the plans for a vehicle it might propel, called it a "road locomotive," and applied for a patent on the combination. He then spent the next sixteen years working to prevent this patent being granted.

Selden's reasons for this seem to have been plausible and honorable enough. He was too poor at the time of his application to build a car and it was too soon to get backers. He wanted, however, to establish priority—hence his application. If the Patent Office had granted the patent then, he could have made no use of it and it might, indeed, have run out before he could capitalize on it. This was a not unrecognized procedure. He could not, however, delay the patent beyond 1895.

Even then he could not get support, and four years later he assigned rights to his patent to the Columbia and Electric Vehicle Company, which at once proceeded to cash in by suing Winton, the principal manufacturer in 1900, for infringement. No effort was made to build a Selden car. It was easier simply to force other builders to pay royalties.

The fact that an American could in 1900 be credited with "inventing" the gasoline automobile shows the prevailing ignorance of the time. Winton's counsel at once claimed that the Selden car was merely a combination of elements already known, patented, and used, but Electric Vehicle won the suit. Intimidated by this victory, Winton and seventeen other manufacturers got together with Electric Vehicle and formed the patent-pooling combination, A.L.A.M., agreeing to pay royalties to the inventor's assignee.

This had happened three months before the Ford Motor Company began. If Ford and his backers knew about it in June, it did not disturb them. In the course of the summer, however, while his other troubles multiplied, it became evident to Ford that the A.L.A.M. meant business. In a Detroit newspaper an advertisement over its imprint stated:

No other manufacturers or importers are authorized to make or sell gasoline automobiles, and any person making, selling or using such machines made or sold by any licensed manufacturers or importers will be liable to prosecution for infringement.

To Ford this was an outrageous interference with the progress of industry. It was also discriminatory. The Association's "Articles of Agreement" specified that no new member could be admitted without the approval of its Board. If the group of manufacturers in the A.L.A.M. decided, therefore, that they wanted no further competition, they could bar any newcomer from the field. As far as Ford himself was concerned, the members with whom he talked were of the opinion that he could not join their little club because he did not manufacture, but merely assembled, motor cars.

Ford did not give them a chance to reconsider this. His reply to the advertisement was not long in coming. It was a notice to "Dealers, Importers, Agents and Users of our Gasoline Automobiles."

We will protect you [it read] against any prosecution for alleged infringement of patents. Regarding the alleged infringement of the Selden patent, we beg to quote the well-known patent attorneys Messrs. Parker and Burton: "The Selden Patent . . . does not cover a practicable machine, no practicable machine can be made from it and never was so far as we can ascertain. . . . None of that type have ever been in use. All have been failures. . . ."

How Ford with his tiny capital proposed to protect his dealers against this powerful organization that threatened to extend its prosecution even to the individual buyers of his cars was probably not clear to him or to Couzens. Evidently he was bluffing, hoping to call the bluff of his opponent. His legal advice suggested that the Selden claims hung on a slender thread—as indeed later developments proved—but the courts had sustained them against Winton and scared eighteen companies, some of them far more solid than Ford's, into paying royalties.

It was, however, a time of business gambling. In a sense, it was a resurgence of pioneering days. The new pioneers were not conquering a frontier of land, but they were advancing one of the great industrial and commercial frontiers of all time. The American people were on the verge of an adventure as exciting and extensive as the treks of the covered wagons or the staking of the gold claims—though none yet knew it—and it would take only the right move to start it. Yet already the tension could be felt by men like Couzens and Ford: the certainty that the stakes were high, worth every risk; the probability that only a few could win and that hundreds would be left by the wayside.

As the fall came on and sales went up—especially in New York City, where the little car was catching on—Ford grew bolder and issued his guarantee with each sale. In October the blow fell. The Electric Vehicle Company, holder of the Selden patent, brought suit against Ford, his eastern distributor, Duerr, and the purchaser of Ford Car No. 134.

It was a bad time for it. The big automobile show was scheduled for January in New York's Madison Square Garden. Already this was the mecca for the trade and the fans, the arena of choice in the fantastic variety of automotive experiment. The A.L.A.M., angered by the Ford advertising, was maneuvering to keep Ford out of the show. If they should succeed, or if prospective customers became intimidated by the example of the threat to the buyer of "No. 134," there would be a speedy end to Malcomson's venture. It was the moment at which, in all its history, the Ford Motor Company most needed a friend.

He appeared, suddenly, in New York. He was a formidable capitalist and merchant whose power lines had moved out from Philadelphia to national celebrity. He was sensitive to the first whispers of mass demand: from the start he had answered with maximum quantity and minimum price. More important still for the moment's need, he loved a fight and he was in command of armies of considerable size to carry it on. His name was John Wanamaker.

Wanamaker seems to have been even surer than Ford himself that Ford was moving in the right direction. He volunteered, in the face of all the threats, for the New York agency. His belief was that Ford, by fighting what he called the "trust," was promoting the whole of the low-priced market because it was obviously in the Selden interest to maintain a high price level. The theory was not wholly borne out, to be sure, by the membership of the A.L.A.M., which included Olds, but it made possible some appealing advertising, which Wanamaker wrote and financed.

The Ford Motor Car [one of these displays proclaimed] cannot be beaten by the Trust, in competition; so they have erected a scarecrow, to frighten the buying public. The smart crow knows that there is always corn where the scarecrow is. . . . *When you buy a Ford Motor Car from John Wanamaker you are guaranteed against any trouble with the trust.*

For the public, the name of Wanamaker carried all the prestige the name of Ford lacked. Wanamaker

also managed to squeeze Ford into the Garden show
—albeit in the basement. Then, four days before the
show opened, Henry Ford himself leaped into the
headlines with the kind of exploit that sent the crowds
pushing their way to his basement booth.

The twelfth of January, 1904, was a bitter day on
Lake St. Clair, northeast of Detroit, and the lake was
frozen solid. Across the ice a straightaway course had
been laid out with a measured mile on it. Snow had
been swept off the track and cinders scattered over it.
These preparations had been made so that Henry
could break the world's speed record for the mile.

He drove the 999, which Barney Oldfield had
made famous two years before. He drove it himself,
with a mechanic named "Spider" Huff blowing into
the tank to keep the gasoline feeding. The time for
the measured mile was 39 ⅖ seconds, just under the
French-held world record. The event, watched by
Clara and ten-year-old Edsel, made a story high in
color and instantly appealing to every adventurous
American. It was both in the Horatio Alger pattern—
the farm boy making good at the risk of his life—and
tuned to the machine thinking of the second industrial
revolution. In these first years of the new century the
United States was swinging into the industrial leadership of the world.

In spite of the threats, then, the new year started
auspiciously. Wanamaker in his turn was sued and
brought legal talent to the battle. The showdown in
the courts was deferred. The interval gave an excellent

chance for the Ford company to build up strength
with the public, which was naturally inclined to lean
toward the underdog, especially when he appeared to
be such a courageous and pugnacious hound and when
his opponent smelled strongly of that great American
bugbear, monopoly. In the end, the A.L.A.M. became one of the greatest assets Ford had—one of the
three or four factors that built his success in the mass
production of automobiles.

Meanwhile, however, radical changes in design
filtered into the American field from overseas. This
trend had, for a moment, an extremely destructive
effect upon the low-priced car that was Ford's dream
and that alone wrought the revolution in American
society and the completion of the continental conquest. The trend may not have begun in January
1904, but it got its greatest impetus from the January
1904 show in the Madison Square Garden.

The story of Henry Ford has been injured both by
mythical adulation and by equally mythical "debunk-
ing." It has often been written with only scant regard
for the technical developments of his time and a failure to understand the workings of a mind whose concentration was primarily technical. Also, the myths on
both sides have often stemmed from a desire to present a consistent picture—all black or all white—of
a man for whom consistency in the constantly alter-
ing days in which he lived was obviously impossible.
It is true that he was stubborn, hard to persuade, some-

times apparently quite madly erratic; yet it was his moments of flexibility, when he recognized—however reluctantly—the external pressures, that assured his ultimate success.

The "Ford-can-do-no-wrong" biographers insist upon the twin impulses of quantity and cheapness as a profound driving force that appeared with their hero's earliest consciousness and from which he never deviated. The debunkers point out many cases in which Ford completely departed from this line, such as when he forgot everything in his supposed passion for racing; when he designed and built several expensive models before his Model T, and when, even after Model T arrived and he stood on the very threshold of success, he seems to have been willing to sell out for cash. Both of these proponents are partly right and both are quite obviously, from the records available to us, partly wrong.

It is hard to deny that Henry Ford was ridden by two obsessions: mechanical perfection and the "common man." Sometimes one of these dominated the other. It is probable that in the years before Model T he was continuously searching for some sort of balance between the concentrations. Perhaps there were fleeting instants when the effort seemed too much for him. We can only guess at the inner workings of his mind, though it is possible that the immense volume of records he has left—only a fraction of which have been explored—will one day show more. In any case, it is fatal to build the story of Henry Ford on any

assumption other than that he was a human being subject to the pitfalls engendered by that peculiar quality
we call genius.

At the automobile show in January 1904 the cyno-
sures for the eyes of the technically minded were the
new foreign cars. The design, perfection of engine
and transmission, solidity, strength of materials, and
general workmanlike appearance of the imported ex-
hibits bewitched these folk and made them ashamed of
the old buggies. It is quite evident from the photographs of American cars of the period that "horselessness" began to disappear from the American scene
precisely in 1904.

Ford saw this. Whatever may have been his later
recorded afterthoughts, it is highly possible that what
ran through his subconscious mind in 1904 was something like this:

"The Ford Model A is obsolete. It no longer even
looks like an automobile. The car of the future must
embody certain new features. It is not possible now to
produce cars with these features at the low price of the
Model A. In time, however, as these things are simplified and standardized, they will grow constantly
cheaper. It is therefore not an abandonment of a 'car
for the masses' to experiment for a time with the more
expensive models. Meanwhile we can sell the Model
A to whoever will buy, build ourselves a backlog,
and then compromise to insure survival in the transition period."

Whether his quick, intuitive mind reached as far

as this in 1904, it is obvious in the light of future events that, if he had then frozen the design of Model A and put it into mass production, it would have fallen into a dated ditch from which nothing could have rescued it. In any case, there is little doubt that in 1904 the technical obsession dominated the mass car in Henry's mind.

In 1905 we see an interesting demonstration of the two obsessions seeking some kind of common level. In that year Ford listed the Model B four-cylinder touring car at $2,000 and the Model C, a two-cylinder four-seater, at $950. It has been said that B was a concession to the stockholders. It is reasonable to suppose that both models were experiments; that Ford, far from being as sure of himself as so many have painted him, was slowly feeling his way, setting up brackets of cost, searching for the answer to large-scale production.

Photographs of these models are revealing. In both, the design has switched over to the foreign principle. The engine has been taken from its alarming position under the seat and set in front beneath a hood. B weighed seventeen hundred pounds, developed twenty horsepower, had a wheelbase of ninety-two inches, automatic oiling, and a three-seat tonneau. C had half the power, but the interesting innovation of a back seat and a side door into it.

For the next three years the models varied from F at $1,200 to K at $2,500. Finally with N and S Henry Ford's experiments ended and he knew what he wanted. From that point in 1907 he hewed to the line and let the chips fall where they might. They certainly fell, fast and thick. But by that time the Ford Motor Company had paid $400,000 in dividends on an original cash investment of $28,000 and Henry Ford was no longer worried about the stability of his concern.

The company's profits had jumped from $283,037 in 1904 to $1,124,675 in 1907. The first dividends in 1903 totaled $12,000. In 1904 they came to $88,000. In the three years, 1905, 1906, and 1907, $100,000 had been paid each year. The net worth of a company capitalized at $100,000 (of which less than a third existed in cash) in June 1903 had become $1,038,822 by October 1907!

IV

MASS production is peculiarly and almost uniquely American in its origins. The main reasons for this are, first: the American belief, in spite of many demonstrations to the contrary, that all men are created equal; and, second: the unparalleled need to supply a constantly migrating and constantly increasing agrarian population with goods produced under an acute labor shortage.

In European and Asiatic societies, tradition prescribed that the best things went to a privileged few. Clocks, watches, fine fabrics, shoes, and, later, sewing machines and bicycles were perquisites of an upper class and filtered slowly, if at all, down to the masses. With abundance of labor many goods could be produced in limited quantities more or less by hand. In the United States, where everyone considered himself "as good as the next man," and where land fever and the pull of the frontier robbed the static centers of skilled workmen, machines had to be designed to multiply the productiveness of a few men and to keep the democracy supplied with what the "inalienable rights" demanded.

Through all of later American history, as social democracy became more and more complete, industry has been continuously occupied in turning luxuries into necessities. Early Connecticut clockmakers made

it possible for timepieces—regarded abroad as prop-
erty of the well-to-do—to become part of the furnishings of the humblest frontier cabins. Machine
production plus installment-selling brought reapers,
harvesters, and threshers to farmers penniless but for
their land. Factory-made shoes and clothing raised the
living standard of American "masses" above that of
other peoples, and, finally, such astonishing luxuries as
electric refrigerators, oil burners, radio, and television
gained markets that to foreigners are truly fabulous.

It is largely to quantity production through semi-
automatic machinery that Americans owe the rapid
development of their country. With the coming of
the twentieth century the enormous territory had been
surprisingly integrated, considering the sparseness of
its population in the frontier period; yet much of the
land was still unexploited, almost unexplored. Cities
and towns followed one another in long, straight lines
along rivers and railroads: to these communities the
rural population had flocked, leaving hundreds of
ghost villages, lonely farms, or large barren stretches
that were virtually wilderness. The railroads had
killed the improvement of highways, and wagon roads
had lapsed into conditions that, a half century later,
are impossible to visualize.

By 1900, however, many Americans had had
glimpses of other horizons. An entirely new taste of
individual freedom—freedom to escape, to explore, to
discover the allures of nature—had come in the nine-
ties with the bicycle. Supposing that the bicycle was

a social fixture, several eager promoters had started
good-roads movements. Imported techniques of road-
building—notably McAdam's—were tried and
proved successful. Finally, in the first year of the new
century, road conditions and the possibilities of new
frontiers in the interior were brought sensationally to
public attention in the exploit of Roy Chapin, who
drove a one-cylinder, curved-dash Oldsmobile buggy
from Detroit to New York. "He was forced," Mr. Arthur Pound tells us, "to leave the muddy highways,
and drive along the towpath of the Erie Canal, con-
testing with mule trains for the right-of-way."

Such things as this undoubtedly sank into the subconscious minds of Americans everywhere and prepared the way for the revolution. It is probable, for
instance, that the great army of boys who followed
automotive development with acute interest saw vi-
sions of their own futures, driving horselessly into far
country. A child taught to believe that he might well
one day become president was still easier to convince
that he might one day drive and even own a car. On
the surface, however, Roy Chapin's feat was regarded as a daring sporting effort—not quite so reck-
less as going over Niagara Falls in a barrel, but in
that general category.

Even six years later, when 142,000 motor vehicles
were registered in the United States, private ownership
of a car was a mark of distinction or, perhaps, evidence of extravagant frivolity: indeed, as we have
seen, business trends seemed to be toward increasing

its luxurious characteristics. Keith Sward, writing of
the early 1900's in *The Legend of Henry Ford*, says:

In this day the rich themselves thought of the automobile as a luxury reserved for the few. . . . It was
understood at the same time that the plain people of the
country were to function as the tenders and repairers of
the motor car. Guided by such a conviction, the Detroit
Saturday Night said in 1909 that the best chauffeurs
were to be recruited from the ranks of former coachmen.
Such drivers, observed the *Saturday Night*, were dutiful
members of the "servant class" who could be counted on
to know "exactly what is expected of them by their
masters."

Whatever may have been Henry Ford's motives
during his company's experimental period, we may be
sure that such statements as this must have exasperated
him. Above all else, this man suspected and despised
the rich and shied away from anything that smacked
of luxury. It would have been wholly out of character for him to favor the production of expensive cars
except for technical purposes. It must, therefore, have
been a satisfaction to him that there was a sharp decline of sales when his $2,500 Model K was intro-
duced and a quick up-curve when the cheaper Model
N went on the market. It was obvious by 1907,
though no suggestion of a "universal car" had yet engaged the public fancy, that the name of Ford was
popularly associated with low-priced automobiles.

We may put our finger precisely on 1907 as the
year in which revolution came. It seems, looking back

on it, as if fate played then into Ford's hands—as if
it were a wind of destiny that shook the stock market
in March, brought the most hopeful securities to the
ground, and sowed the seeds of October panic. The
rich were hard hit. Low-priced cars were more than
ever sought after. In the course of the year Ford production jumped to about eighty-five hundred, five
times that of the previous year; and the great bulk of
it consisted of the latest experimental light cars—
Models N, R, and S, all selling for less than $1,000.

Watching these things, keeping careful track of
costs, thinking of the future in terms of expansion beyond all dreams of the time in this first adolescence of
the industry, Henry Ford evolved his great concept.
It was in the light of this vision that he felt too confined in the Piquette-Beaubien plant, to which the
company had moved when Strelow's Mack Avenue
shop would no longer hold it. He planned for the
purchase of the sixty-acre Highland Park race track,
where he talked of building "the largest automobile
factory in the world."

Various employees of the Ford Motor Company
have claimed credit for the revolutionary idea. It has
been said that it was not one man's brainstorm, but
the result of the focusing of many minds. It is undoubtedly true that others contributed details of design and, especially, production methods. But no one
can examine the records or analyze the reminiscences
of Ford workers of the period without knowing beyond question not only that Henry Ford's was the

master mind but that the whole of the broad project originated with him. Indeed, we find evidence of discontented and sometimes angry rumblings throughout the time when the plan was taking shape and, indeed, of the disgusted exit of two of the most important production men in the plant. And with Ford's contemplation of the new gigantic installations at Highland Park—to be financed entirely by the plowing back of profits—the waves of unrest spread out to the stockholders. So the project had far from unanimous support.

The project was Model T.

The way for the realization of Model T was now open. If the idea had occurred to Henry Ford before —as it probably had—there were difficulties to be overcome. He had not had full control. Malcomson, with whom he had shared equally the majority stockholding, was opposed to concentrating on a low-priced car. But here too the gods were conniving. Malcomson had sold out to Ford. Speculating in other directions, he had needed cash and, as the stock for which he had originally paid $12,000 was now worth $175,000, he was content. Albert Strelow and three minor stockholders had followed Malcomson's exit. Ford bought all of these shares. Those who like to play the game known as "the if's of history" enjoy speculating on the millions these men might have made had they remained aboard. Yet if they had stuck, perhaps there would have been no Model T. Poor

Strelow put the $25,000 he received into a gold mine, which almost immediately turned out to be barren, and he was later reported standing in line for a lowly job with the company he had once partly owned.

By 1907, then, 58½ shares of stock in the Ford Motor Company had been acquired by Henry Ford, giving him full power in the management of the company. In these fateful years some valuable technical assets had also arrived. To make crankshafts for Model N, Ford had hired a great, brawny, uncouth ox of a man named Walter Flanders, who, nevertheless, was original, ingenious, and highly versed in mass-production techniques. Also, working creatively in the company since 1904, another giant, physically and mentally, was a Dane named Charles Sorensen or "Cast-iron Charlie." This man, whose later contributions to the moving assembly were perhaps without equal anywhere, was an old friend of Henry's going back to the days of the Edison company. A third was the brilliant mechanic, P. Edward ("Pete") Martin.

These men and others picked by the chief's almost infallible instinct must, by the methods of economy and speed they installed—rearranging machinery, devising jigs and fixtures for accurate machine-tool work, dividing labor, and insisting on interchangeability—have led Ford over the months into his large, over-all view of the most adaptable product for full mass production. He was constantly moving through all the departments, watching every man and every machine. Like Frederick Taylor, the great inventor of scientific management, Ford had a passion for simplifying operations, for economy of time and materials, for eliminating little waste motions from each worker's performance.

It is remarkable how close all this came to the carefully worked-out plans of Taylor, because Ford had certainly not read Taylor's treatises. It must be assumed that the efficiency patterns came into the Ford plant with the factory men he hired, but in the use of them Ford exercised a critical judgment and creative force that everyone acknowledged. His power lay in an instant recognition of what was right and what was wrong in any new method. The reminiscences of the workers taken, after Ford's death, on tape recordings testify to the master's almost constant pressure, walking over miles of factory floor, stopping at every work center to watch or speak, to say no, to nod approval, to berate—perhaps fire on the spot—an inflexible, perverse, or skeptical worker. A man in these times who hinted, even by the expression of his face, that he thought one of the master's schemes impossible was doomed.

Mr. Ford [Charles Sorensen recalls] never caught me saying that an idea he had couldn't be done. If I had the least idea that it couldn't be done, I wouldn't announce myself on it to him. . . . I always felt the thing would prove itself.

Walter Flanders thought the Model T project was impossible. He did not think the Model T itself was impossible. He was willing to try that. But he thought the *project* would be fatal to the company. He thought Ford was crazy to pursue it and said so. He then walked out before Ford had a chance to invite his departure.

It was not Ford's determination to produce Model T—a simple, sturdy, utilitarian, low-priced job— that worried Flanders. It was his determination *to produce nothing but*. It was a profound obsession in the industry that no manufacturer could survive concentrating on a single model—that he must offer a choice and make annual changes. Today we may sympathize with this view. The industrialists of 1907 were merely thinking twenty years ahead of their time. Mass production of this highly complex machine had to be established first—not only technically but economically as well. We know now that a Model T project had to be injected into American society before the universal market and the universal desire could become facts. The *flexible* mass production that engineers are dreaming of in the 1950's will probably follow more flexible tastes of the future. But *inflexible* mass production had to precede it: neither the techniques nor the popular demand of the years immediately following 1907 would have permitted anything else. That was the fact: but of all the eager folk who were then engaged in pushing the horse off the American road, only Henry Ford knew it.

Against the advice, then, of those who should have known better—yet who, curiously enough, provided

many of the technical needs of the scheme—Henry
Ford announced that thereafter there would be only
one Ford.

> I will build a motor car [he stated] for the great multi-
> tude. It will be large enough for the family but small
> enough for the individual to run and care for. It will be
> constructed of the best materials, by the best men to be
> hired, after the simplest designs that modern engineering
> can devise. But it will be so low in price that no man
> making a good salary will be unable to own one—and
> enjoy with his family the blessing of hours of pleasure
> in God's great open spaces.

Advertising men have done a great deal of talking
about "psychology" and much solemn experimenting
with it. Yet it would be hard to find in all their copy
anything as appealing in its time as this simple, almost
biblically worded statement. What American before
1910 could be indifferent to the vision of transporting
his family, of a Sunday or holiday, into "God's great
open spaces"? What head of a family would not be
inflated by the prospect of running and caring for this
family machine? What "equal" citizen would admit
to making anything less than a "good salary"?

In his autobiography Ford recalls that his rivals
were delighted by this announcement and by the news
that he had bought the sixty acres at Highland Park
for his production. The question, he says, asked so
many thousand times since, was already being asked
in 1908 and 1909: "How soon will Ford blow up?"

It is asked [he adds] only because of the failure to grasp that a principle rather than an individual is at work, and the principle is so simple that it seems mysterious.

The principle was to decide on your design, freeze it, and, from then on, spend all your time, effort, and money on making the machinery to produce it—concentrating so completely on production that, as volume goes up, it is certain to get cheaper per unit produced. Changing your design every year means retooling your factory every year; it means not continuing one process long enough to study ways of making it more economical; it means constantly changing your orders for materials; it means that the customers have to learn new tricks; it means that salesmen have to keep changing their story; it means expensive advertising.

The "great multitude," Ford thought, was not interested in fashions or experiments; it did not care about pretty lines or colors in a car: it wanted something useful to drive to town or country, something that would meet any road conditions, something that took no thought to drive, no expense to maintain, no special skill to repair. And the multitude, Ford believed, *would want these things forever* and nothing else. This was the theory and philosophy of mass production carried to its extreme.

Workers still living remember Ford in his elation, the almost fanatical excitement of his drive as this concept came to full flower in his mind. He would look at the design for a cylinder block or differential or steering unit and say: "There! We won't change that until we've built a hundred thousand cars!" At the beginning he wanted to simplify the manufacture until skilled workers were eliminated—until, as one pattern-maker remembers, "he just took a man off the street and broke him in like a piece of machinery doing a certain job." This was not an effort to get cheap labor. It was simply that, for the tremendous production that he envisioned, there was not enough skilled labor in the world; also, production could never become fast enough until the worker's motions were almost automatic and without thought.

The idea of Model T jelled in 1907, machinery for production was built in 1908, actual production began in 1909. If we look at the production figures for the calendar years, we will see a drop of about two thousand in 1908 while old models were being disposed of and the "revolution" prepared.

The company's production for 1907 was 8,423. For 1908 it was 6,158. In 1909, after the launching of Model T, it jumped to 12,292; a year later it was 19,293. From then on, figures for the calendar years and their acceleration from year to year were, in the eyes of other manufacturers, "astronomical."

In 1908 Detroiters watched with amazement the excavations and construction at the Highland Park race track. The idea that anything as big as this could be dedicated to anything as restricted in sales appeal as an automobile seemed pure fantasy to wise, conservative businessmen, and many a head was shaken as the huge buildings went up.

In 1908, too, there would be a little gathering on the third floor of the Piquette-Beaubien plant every Sunday. Sorensen would be there with some of his most imaginative assistants, moving piles of materials about the floor to figure out the most efficient means of assembling a car. Ford would usually be there watching. He was not an inventor of the detail of these techniques. But he could spot quickly a right or wrong method. Again and again he would say: "No, no! Not fast enough! That won't produce enough cars. When we get into production we must have twenty-five thousand within twelve months."

Perhaps even Ford himself would not have believed then that within three years Model T would be rolling out at the average rate of well over three thousand cars a month—better than forty thousand in the course of a year!

It was at about this time that Ford put to use in the Model T one of his greatest technical discoveries. This was vanadium steel. Ford had started his inquiry on this three years before.

In 1905 I was at a motor race at Palm Beach. There was a big smashup and a French car was wrecked. . . . I thought the foreign cars had smaller and better parts than we knew anything about. After the wreck I picked up a little valve strip stem. It was very light and very strong. I asked what it was made of. Nobody knew. I gave the stem to my assistant.

"Find out all about this," I told him. "That is the kind of material we ought to have in our cars."

The assistant found that the piece was made of an alloy of steel and vanadium—a relatively rare metal —and Ford then found that no one in America knew how to make it commercially. He sent to England for a metallurgical engineer who did know, had him instruct a small Ohio steel company. He had to guarantee this company against loss: then, after one abortive try, it turned out the steel. It had a tensile strength of 170,000 pounds compared with 60,000 and 70,000 in the steel he had been using.

The vanadium steel [Ford explained in his autobiography] disposed of much of the weight. The other requisites of a universal car I had already worked out and many of them were in practice. The design had to balance. Men die because a part gives out. Machines wreck themselves because some parts are weaker than others. . . . Also [the car] had to be fool proof. This was difficult because a gasoline motor is essentially a delicate instrument and there is a wonderful opportunity for anyone who has a mind that way to mess it up. I adopted this slogan:

"When one of my cars breaks down I know I am to blame."

Through all of the intense period of preparation we feel—over every record and yarn, every cold fact and warm anecdote—an unmistakable aura of success. After the announcement of Model T, orders began to pour in: before the year was over it was necessary for headquarters to notify dealers that "there will be no use of your taking any more orders as we, under no circumstances can enter them here." Thus the appearance was a business utopia, a seller's market, a demand far beyond the supply, and money rolling in. What was there to worry about?

Behind the scene there was a great deal. Again Ford was aware of the cool shadow of the sword over his head—the threat, deferred, postponed, half forgotten in the full years, of the Selden patent. If Ford lost the suit that was pending, more than half a million might have to go for past royalties.

When the Association of Licensed Automobile Manufacturers had been formed to pay Selden royalties, Ford had not been invited to join. Later a formal invitation had been extended and he and his business manager, Couzens, had refused so angrily that the Selden people had promised to get even. Now when the horizons were bright, new threats were coming by mail and telephone to the Ford offices. Large display advertisements were appearing, warning the buyers of Ford cars. "Don't buy a lawsuit with your car" was the slogan calculated to frighten the prospective customers.

Ford and Couzens stuck to their guns. They offered to post a bond with each purchaser for his protection. Nevertheless, it seems likely that they were deeply disturbed. It is said to have cost the company some $200,000 to defend itself against the attacks. These worries have furnished the only adequate reason given by any of Ford's biographers for two extraordinary incidents that occurred in 1908 and 1909.

The principal in both of these was the promoter of General Motors, William C. Durant, a highly romantic character given to sensational speculative plunges. In 1908, before General Motors, when, perhaps, he was feeling his way toward that concept, he made a proposition to Ford. How about a merger, he suggested, of Buick (which he controlled), Maxwell-Briscoe, Reo (the company Ransom Olds had formed when he left Oldsmobile), and Ford? It would probably have surprised no one if Ford had refused outright—it would indeed have been in character. But he did not refuse. He listened. Finally he agreed, if Durant would pay three million dollars entirely in cash instead of partly in stock. It is probable that Durant could have raised the money, in which case the Ford Motor Company would have been submerged. At this point, however, Olds followed Ford's lead, made the same demand, and the deal fell through.

In 1909, a Federal court sustained the validity of the Selden patent. Shortly afterward Durant, who in the meantime had established General Motors, came back with an offer to buy the Ford Motor Company outright for eight million—two million of which was to be in money. Again Ford demanded the full sum in cash on the barrelhead. The bankers to whom Durant applied for this money told him the Ford Company "was not worth that much," and again the negotiations collapsed.

Certain of Ford's critics have accused him of greed for money in these abortive deals, saying that money meant more to him than his industrial career. There is abundant evidence, apart from the celebrated story of Clara's finding a forgotten fifty-thousand-dollar check in one of Henry's forgotten trouser pockets, that this was not true. The incidents must, therefore, be put down to those imponderables of temperament that are human weaknesses as well as the properties of genius—coupled with exasperation over the continuous Selden pressure.

It was Henry Ford's variations from a norm, rather than his conformity to a standard or code, that made him both feared and loved, and that, for many generations to come, will probably cause speculation and wonder about a character who stands so conspicuously in the foreground of American folklore.

The long Selden fight came to an end on January 9, 1911, with a decision by the Circuit Court of Appeals. The validity of the patent was upheld, but the court maintained that it covered only vehicles propelled by the Brayton type of engine. As Ford cars were propelled by an engine of the Otto type, it was held that Ford had not infringed. Since the Otto type

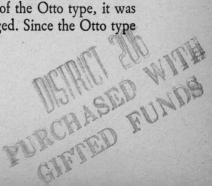

was being used by every other American manufacturer, it turned out that no one had infringed and the
A.L.A.M. automatically ceased to exist. The decision
signalized one of the greatest victories of Henry Ford's
career and an incalculable boon to the whole American industry.

V

IN exploring history, it is always engaging to discover
the narrow escapes by which our destinies have survived. That the Ford Motor Company came so near
being overwhelmed by forces with quite different
directions, yet rode over the hump, seems, as we read
of it, largely a matter of luck. Yet there are those who
believe with William Bolitho that men of powerful
will unconsciously turn what we call fate into an
instrument for their own purposes. It is possible that
Henry Ford knew by that mysterious insight he so
often demonstrated that his own terms of sale would be
refused and that he felt satisfaction in the naming of a
prohibitive price. In any case he came out, after
Durant's second attempt, with the announcement
that:

Folks that have wanted to buy out Ford have not
been able to talk in cash, although the paper figures might
be high.

We may guess that, if the sale had taken place, the
"universal car" that Model T turned out to be would
have been delayed. It was the special set of conditions under which Ford's team worked—the concentration on a single model, the preoccupation with
simplification, the purchase of the best materials at a
big-quantity price—that made "Lizzie" the rugged

little pioneer she was, able to create a whole new pattern of communications over "impassable" roads. It took Ford himself to insist on Lizzie's ugliness, her respectability, her black, workaday, middle-class Americanism, the fascination of an engine and "works" that could be fixed by any adolescent farm lad between milking and haying. Into Lizzie went a part of Ford himself: his contempt for wealth and show and servants, his rustic-bred pride in independence, his unarticulated belief in equality of opportunity, his toughness of will. It was these specific things that, for the first time, took the automobile out of the luxury class—turned the rich man's toy into the plain man's utility.

Where Lizzie went in those first days, she became a member of the family. She shared with the farmer the rough honesty, the willingness to get calluses, so to speak, on her hands and hayseeds or manure dust into her lungs. Lizzie was a pet, she had personality: in spite of the standardized, interchangeable elements in her assembly she became temperamental, individual, and "ornery." Jones's Lizzie coughed differently from Robinson's Lizzie; the shift of her planetaries screeched a different complaint; she acquired a port instead of a starboard list as leaves split in her springs; cylinders one and three in Jones's Lizzie were the silent ones, whereas two and four in Robinson's failed to catch, and the galloping consumption in Smith's carburetor gave him a new topic of conversation with Huggins down the road, who had mended a break in his distributor with a safety pin and had forgotten to replace it with a "boughten" part.

The machines were, of course, immensely sensitive to individual handling. The use of haywire, five-and-ten bolts, bent nails, fish-line, and clippings from copper chimney flashing all transferred to Lizzie certain whims of her owner. There were few repair mechanics in the early days of Model T and no standardized garage procedure. In those days a generation of amateur mechanics grew into American society: men and the sons of men who, when war came, could invent on the spur of the moment a score of gadgets for survival. The great legend of "Yankee ingenuity" —supposed to have been innate since colonial days— was largely a result of Model T's invasion of the backwoods.

It was the meeting, then, of a surge of desire— hitherto groping and uncertain but sweeping the country like wind—with the perfect answer, the complete fulfillment, that made flivver ways into true American folkways. The T was indigenous in its time, grassroots American; as Yankee-scented as the potbellied stove sizzling with true-aimed tobacco juice. In the second decade of the twentieth century it led the way to the physical America we know: laboriously, noisily, but infallibly, in those years it was laying out the concrete network of the new continent, and in most of that time it was doing it unaided.

The roads followed after the Ford car [remembers one of the early dealers]. Ford took the lead because it alone could survive the roads of the time. . . . The transverse springs and planetary gears provided traction where other cars bucked. We could take ruts, chuck-holes, anything.

Early in the Model T's career, corner-grocery wit began to work on it. A man about to die (they told, sitting round the cracker barrel) had one deathbed request. He asked that his Ford be buried with him, because he had never been in a hole yet that his Ford didn't get him out of. And so on into a volume of tales and anecdotes so varied and colorful that Henry decided to let it save him countless millions in adver-tising. The jokes may have helped. But the Model T sold itself. The dealers did not have to "follow up" their "prospects." The potential customers pursued the dealers, clamoring for delivery.

The new Highland Park plant opened on the day after New Year's, 1910. It was none too soon. In the calendar year 1909 more than twelve thousand cars had been produced and the Piquette-Beaubien plant had burst its seams. Cars and machinery had spilled out and operations of assembly were carried on out of doors. As the huge outlay was moved and installed in the new buildings it was necessary to make innovations in production methods; otherwise the thousands of calls from every corner of the country could never have been answered.

There was room to move at Highland Park, and continuous movement was the steady aim of Ford's engineers. The growth, step by step, of automotive mass production as it developed at Highland Park over the next five years is deeply fascinating to any student of this extraordinary American symphony, but only a few "leitmotivs," so to speak, that originated with him can be played in the story of Henry Ford. Harmony and counterpoint were worked out by others.

1. The work must be brought to the man; not the man to the work. The old plan by which a car frame remained static in one place while workmen ran about the shop for parts to attach to it was forever scrapped. The frame must move from one team of men to another, and each team must be continuously supplied by other moving lines with the parts it is expected to attach. Thus evolved the main or final moving assembly line with many sub-assemblies moving into it. Along the sub-assemblies motors, springs, steering units, bodies, were put together, the "main component" of each sliding along—by gravity, if possible— on slanted chutes from team to team and being worked on, a little at a time, the workers adding something here and there until the unit was complete and could be carried to the main assembly, where ran the endless line of partly finished cars.

2. The work must be brought to the man *waist-high*. No worker must ever have to stoop to attach a wheel, bolt, screw, or anything else to the moving chassis.

These two basic principles were fundamental to Ford assembly. It took about seven years from the first

experiments to get the full complex into smooth working order. At Highland Park they began with a minor
sub-assembly: the fly-wheel magneto. It had been
customary for one man to do the entire job of assembling a magneto. It had taken him twenty minutes.
Ford split the work into twenty-nine operations, had
the growing magneto carried through them on a conveyor, and the assembly time was cut to four minutes.

Ford himself described the main assembly line, on
which there were forty-five operations:

The first men fasten four mudguard brackets to the
chassis frame; the motor arrives on the tenth operation
and so on in detail. Some men do only one or two operations, others do more. The man who places a part does
not fasten it—the part may not be fully in place until
after several operations later. The man who puts in a bolt
does not put on the nut; the man who puts on the nut
does not tighten it. On operation number thirty-four the
budding motor gets its gasoline . . . on operation
number forty-four the radiator is filled with water, and
on operation number forty-five the car drives out. . . .

To carry out all of this plan it was necessary to ar-
range machines in new sequences. Before, similar
machines had been grouped together: drills in one
place, borers in another, millers in another, and so on.
Ford changed all this. If a sequence of operations
called for it, a miller would stand next a drill press
and even an annealing oven would be injected into a
line of machine tools. This called for radical innovations in the application of power—greatly simplified

when individual electric motors replaced cumbersome shafts and belting.

For some time before 1910 Ford had concentrated more and more manufacture in his own shop. He did not believe in this, but he found it necessary. The ideal, he thought, was to have parts made by different plants all over the country and contracted for by the assembler—the system, in short, with which he had begun. But he had found that outside companies were far behind him in concepts of economy, that their materials were inferior, their deliveries uncertain. So by 1910 most of the Model T was made at home, but bought parts like tires were unpacked, put on overhead conveyors, and carried to the main assembly along with the parts Ford's own machines had made.

The result of all this mechanization and minute division of labor was, of course, that scarcely any real skill was required in the making of a Model T except among the top engineers who designed the processes.

As to machinists, [wrote Arnold and Faurote in their classic volume, *Ford Methods and Ford Shops*] old time, all-round men, perish the thought! The Ford Company has no use for experience, in the working ranks anyway. It desires and prefers machine-tool operators who have nothing to unlearn, who . . . will simply do as they are told to do, over and over again, from bell-time to bell-time. . . .

As mechanization became more and more complete, howls of protest arose over the "stultifying"

monotony of the endless repetition in the work. It is
probable that the complaints came more frequently
from shocked sociologists than from the assembly-
line workers, but, with the general spreading of the
horror that sensitive human beings with eternal souls
should be put to such slow torture, Ford employees
began to drop off at an alarming rate—many of them
finding work among rival automobile companies in
Detroit, the city that was rapidly becoming the automotive center of the world. This happened after the
moving assembly was working in 1913. On the fifth
of January, 1914, Henry Ford made a gesture that
brought him into the headlines of newspapers all over
the world. It became for weeks almost the only topic
of conversation among businessmen. Clergymen
preached of it on Sundays. There was wide speculation as to whether Ford was a saint or insane. It was
unheard of, unprecedented. It was the beginning of
industrial disaster—or the start of millennium.

In fact, it was neither unheard of nor unprecedented—except, perhaps, in degree. Observers of the
industrial scene had talked about the monotony of
repetition ever since Adam Smith, and it had increased
with every stage of mechanized quantity production.
It had simply been carried to an "unprecedented"
extreme in the Ford plant. Henry Ford's sudden act
of compensation was by no means unheard of. In his
Principles of Scientific Management, published in
1911, Frederick Winslow Taylor had written:

The *management* must also recognize the broad fact that workmen will not submit to this more rigid standardization . . . unless they receive extra pay for doing it.

Yet when Henry Ford announced on January 5, 1914, that he was establishing throughout his plant a minimum wage of five dollars a day he became overnight a hero and a villain.

It is true that in the "taylorized" industries the pay rise had been more gradual. It is true that a good many industrialists had repudiated "taylorization" and called Taylor a crackpot. It is also true that, though his plan had been widely adopted, it had not become "news."

By 1914, however, "Tin Lizzie" had carried Ford's name far and wide. For Model T alone he was regarded as something of a benefactor—especially as the price had dropped from $950 in 1909 to $600 in 1913. Now, with the announcement that he had *more than doubled* the minimum wage in his factory, it was natural that the newspaper make-up men picked their largest type to blazon it to the world.

Ford was given full credit for the idea. Businessmen said that none of his subordinates would be mad enough to think of such a thing: that here was another demonstration of the kind of independence of sound business judgment that would eventually wreck him.

Actually, according to most authorities, the five-dollar day came about in this way:

James Couzens, the business manager, had during 1913 become deeply disturbed by the large labor turnover as well as by the attempted invasion of Highland Park by a labor organization known as the International Workers of the World. Theodore Mac-Manus, accepted by many as an expert historian of the early American automobile industry, goes to a sentimental extreme in crediting Couzens with emotional distress over conditions of labor in general. In any case, it seems to have been Couzens who first suggested the five-dollar day, and it required considerable argument to induce Ford to agree.

It is probable that Ford came round partly in advance contemplation of the explosion the gesture would cause. He liked explosions. He liked attacks by his competitors. He also liked to be regarded as the friend of labor. But it is also probable that he saw in Couzens's suggestion the chance of getting more work from his men by paying them a higher wage. This motive has been roundly condemned, though why an employer of labor should not feel justified in expecting more work for more money is not clear. Finally, Ford saw—as he himself has stated—the certainty of building a new market for his car among his own employees. Ford did not admit Couzens's part in the five-dollar day, but he did more than once avow that the profit motive had much to do with it.

Among labor itself the move had some truly terrible repercussions. The sudden news brought ten thousand job-hunters from all over the country to the Highland Park gates. A Detroit winter is not a comfortable setting for such a gathering. The week of the announcement was a peculiarly bitter one. When word reached the huge crowd that, naturally, there were not jobs for ten thousand newcomers, a riot started. There is no doubt that the company should have made provision for this result and for the orderly handling of applicants, but apparently no one had thought of that, expecting only sweetness and light to surround the generous gesture. The ultimate tragedy came when, at their wits' end, the local police turned freezing water from a fire hose upon the unhappy crowd.

Later it was said that all Ford workers did not in fact get the minimum wage, that work was increased to a point where it turned hundreds of workers into nervous wrecks, and that the assembly lines had been speeded up to the point of nightmare. Like so many of the stories, good or bad, that were told about this fabled company, these reports were often exaggerated. Engineers who have studied large moving assembly complexes know, for instance, that to speed up a main assembly you have to speed up a dozen sub-assemblies at the same time and that some of them are not subject to quickening. Acceleration must, therefore, be gradual—not an overnight performance, as was charged. Also, every industrial engineer knows that sudden speed-ups result in expensive spoiled work. Nevertheless, that creeping, endless conveyor belt with its line of growing chassis inevitably lends itself to the picture, and the picture is difficult to erase.

Some analysts of Ford's character think that he became so inflated by the publicity attending the five-dollar day that from then on his arrogance mounted; that what humility he had vanished; that he became, inwardly, as ruthless as his machines while outwardly he maintained the gentle smile of a great benefactor of mankind.

Yet some eighteen months later he made another gesture that in its naïve faith was positively mystic. Whatever has been said of his business cynicism, his insincerity, his double-dealing, or his greed—and there have been occasions that supported each of these charges—his critics are usually baffled by the events of late 1915. There may have been crackpot delusions of power, but there was no profit motive in the impulse that resulted in the pilgrimage of the *Oscar II*.

From the outbreak, in Europe, of the First World War, Ford had grown increasingly pacifist. His particular kind of success had depended on a free economy impossible in wartime. The interest in the country's development that Model T's exploits had aroused in him was sincere; it was unbearable to him that this progress should be interrupted. He had the aloof contempt that most citizens of what was then an isolationist stronghold felt for European politics. Finally, he had a very genuine hatred of killing in any form and, not having the equipment for the historical analysis of international behavior, the normal performance of an army was, to him, just plain murder.

His opinions were known to several prominent pacifists of the time. David Starr Jordan and Louis

Lochner were anxious for the United States to carry
on "continuous mediation" in Europe and, when
President Wilson was cool to this proposal, they
looked for a millionaire to finance a publicity campaign for the project. The Hungarian pacifist Rosika
Schwimmer had already gained Ford's ear on the subject and when—after several luncheon meetings, in
which Lochner and Mme Schwimmer were joined
by Jane Addams, Oswald Garrison Villard, and a
number of educators, editors, and clergymen—it was
suggested that American delegates to a neutral commission in Europe proceed by special ship, Ford announced that he would finance the expedition.

If I can be of any service whatever [he said] in help-
ing end this war and keeping America out of it, I shall
do it if it costs me every dollar and every friend I have.

He tried, personally, to persuade the President to
give the pilgrimage official sanction and, upon Wilson's natural refusal, he released the full story to the
press, with appalling results. Whether or not Ford
himself made the promise to "get the boys out of the
trenches by Christmas," the slogan was roundly ridi-
culed by the newspapers of the country—especially
as November was then already well advanced.

The *Oscar II*, chartered by Ford, was scheduled to
sail on December 4. In the weeks before the sailing a
corps of stenographers in the Biltmore Hotel in New
York who had sent out invitations to the voyage were
busy opening declinations. Persons Ford and Mme

Schwimmer had counted on sent late regrets: Bryan, Edison, John Burroughs, Ida Tarbell, and others. But the Biltmore suite was besieged, as Mark Sullivan tells, by "star-eyed enthusiasts as well as cranks, fanatics, butters-in and joy-rider of all sorts." And the reporters, the newspaper wags, the cartoonists were everywhere. "It was the answer," Walter Millis writes, "to an editor's prayer," and he adds:

The famous "Peace Ship" had been launched, to the undying shame of American journalism, upon one vast wave of ridicule.

Other writers have since thought the laughter of the press shameful. Yet at the time, with the widespread pro-Allies feeling following upon the sinking of the *Lusitania* in May, and as some of the incidents of the preparation were unmistakably absurd, the often cruel laughter could hardly have been avoided. The American press is rarely gentle with such naïve idealism.

The *Oscar II* left on the fourth in a chaos that has repeatedly been described as "indescribable," with every sort of comedian on the dock and Henry Ford standing at the rail waving quite seriously and throwing American Beauty roses to the crowd. The whole affair was undoubtedly insulting to our future allies, thousands of whose young men were dying daily in the worst possible conditions of filth and horror. Its planlessness, its hurried, haphazard organization, its execrable publicity have since been thought by many earnest and intelligent pacifists to have put a stop to any possible peace movements later in the war. Yet, in retrospect, there is something deeply moving about the impulses behind it. Twenty-five years later, as William Simonds tells in his biography of Ford, the *Detroit Free Press*, on the December anniversary, said editorially:

But we do not laugh any more, nor joke, when that unique argosy is mentioned. We mourn rather the disappearance of times when men could still believe in progress in human enlightenment, and thought that even those in the throes of blood lust might be led to reason. . . .

No peace ship has sailed since the Second World War began. It could find no port either geographically or in the hearts of men.

In the Ford party was one who was strongly opposed to the whole affair. This was a prominent and intelligent clergyman, Dean Marquis, of Detroit's Episcopal cathedral. Marquis, a friend of the Ford family and Mrs. Ford's spiritual adviser, had left the church in order to accept employment in the company. At the request of Mrs. Ford and several of the company's executives he had pleaded with Ford not to go on the Peace Ship. It had been useless, so Marquis went along, hoping to persuade him to leave the pilgrimage and come back as soon as possible. His opportunity came when Ford, drenched by a wave on deck, got a severe cold and was confined to his stateroom. Marquis invaded it and again brought his persuasion to bear.

Until the party landed in Norway, however, Ford was adamant. In Christiania he added to his cold by insisting on walking to the hotel through a snowstorm. Finally, weak and tired, he gave in and admitted to Louis Lochner: "I guess I had better go home to mother. You've got this thing started now and can go along without me."

They went—to Stockholm, Copenhagen, and The Hague—and elected a permanent delegation, which Ford continued to finance until the break with Germany in 1917.

Ford returned to Detroit, where at the moment his company was producing two thousand Model T's a day. Late in the year the millionth Ford car had come off the line. Nothing quite like this production had ever been seen in the industrial history of the world.

Samuel Simpson Marquis, who for years had held Detroit Episcopal congregations spellbound with his sermons, was Ford's choice to head the "Sociological Department" of the company, established after the five-dollar day was in force. This was an experiment in paternalism. If men were to receive this tremendous wage, they must be taught how to spend it properly—not in dissipation and extravagant living. Ford was a militant anti-alcohol and anti-tobacco enthusiast, and for a while it was reported that a man would be fired if the smell of liquor was detected on his breath or if he smoked on duty. The Sociological Department tried to control these matters in the men's homes as well as in the plant.

A worker recalls the workings of this division:

They had a group of men on their staff that went out and checked all the employees. It was a door check. They went out to the home and they had a regular form that they filled out. They picked on your life history; how you lived and where you went to church and everything.

They went to my house. My wife told them everything. There was nothing to keep from them. Of course there was a lot of criticism. . . . It was kind of a funny idea in a free state.

The idea in back of it was to help the people. . . . It was to educate people how to keep on living without getting money-foolish.

The idea eventually was so harshly criticized that it was abandoned. Yet even so stern a critic of Ford as Keith Sward admits in his *Legend of Henry Ford* the value of the institution.

On the positive side [Sward writes], the men who worked [in the Department] helped to "Americanize" Ford's vast body of immigrant workmen. Their charges were encouraged to start savings accounts and to budget their incomes. They were given elementary lessons in hygiene and home management. The wives of many of the foreign born were taught how to shop to the best advantage and how to distinguish between various cuts of meat.

There is little doubt that the project was benevolent in intent. But abuses crept in. The social workers were accused of spying and getting members of a family to give evidence against one another. Perhaps the news, as the war went on, of German paternalism, called "tyranny," increased the adverse feeling. In any case, the scheme was given up, and it is possible that Marquis—who afterward wrote one of the most intelligent interpretations of Ford ever made—was relieved to see the last of it. Its place was taken by the installation, with equally benevolent intent and more lasting results, of the Ford trade schools for boys.

The war increased the tension between Ford and the press and between Ford and some of his associates. We have seen some of this in his altercation with the *Chicago Tribune* in the summer of 1916 due to his anti-militaristic attitude toward the Mexican Border patrol. As much as a year before this, however, before the Peace Ship, Ford's violent objection to America's taking part in the war even to the extent of "preparedness" brought to a head his long-smoldering disagreements with James Couzens. In October 1915 Couzens had resigned.

He had objected to Ford's statements on peace given to reporters. He had been strongly opposed to articles in the company's house organ against preparedness and to large newspaper advertisements, paid for by the company, in which similar views were expressed.

I could not agree [Couzens stated] with Mr. Ford's utterances. . . .

I disapprove of his views on preparedness, and it was of so serious moment to me that I decided to break relations with him. The friendly relations that have existed between us for years have been changed of late, our disagreements daily becoming more violent.

I finally decided that I would not be carried along on that kind of a kite. We started in the automobile business thirteen years ago and it was through my efforts that the Ford Motor Company was built up around one man— Henry Ford.

I have never in my life worked for any man. . . . I will be willing to work with Henry Ford, but I refuse to work for him.

Ford's contention was that Couzens had political ambitions to which the Ford views on war and peace were hurtful, and it is true that Couzens later became a senator. However, from this point on, more and more separations occurred between Ford and his old associates. On both sides there was discontent. Ford came to hold his minority stockholders in contempt as absentee owners and "parasites," and events moved the company ever closer to one-man dictatorship.

It is curious that—in spite of this authoritarian leaning; in spite of ruthless dealings with supply companies and small businesses; in spite of the trends of his behavior alternately toward the twin American bugbears, socialism and monopoly—Ford's popularity with the rank and file of the American people never waned. Through all the ridicule and bitter condemnation of large sections of the press, through scathing in-dictments in the courts, and despite his lack of "pa-triotism" on the threshold of war, he remained what Sward calls a "folk-hero" all his life and, since his death, has been enshrined as such in American popu-lar memory.

VI

THE LAST years of World War I saw the strangest series of happenings in all of Henry Ford's life. It seemed as if he had moved his foot rapidly from one pedal to another of a Model T, causing full stops, reverses, and high speeds ahead in quick succession. To businessmen and financiers it was anyone's guess which way he would jump next. To the press he was a fountainhead of sensational copy, even when the war news was hot and heavy. To the general public everything he did was good—or at least "smart"—and the Ford legend grew apace. In the smoking compartments of Pullmans, on the vaudeville stage, even in pulpits, the Ford jokes multiplied. The jokes made fun of Model T, but they were rarely bitter: sometimes they were given political or other topical application.

At about the same time that the *Chicago Tribune* faced the libel suit for calling him an anarchist, Henry gave pointed evidence of socialistic leanings. He announced that he would cut dividends to the bone and put the bulk of the company's profits into, first, reducing the price of Model T; second, enormously expanding his plant. Except for himself, he said, the stockholders were non-producers, their fat dividends were unearned; profit should go to the workers and the work; for the good of the country more men

should be given jobs; the "money power" was a
menace. These were a few of the remarks that must
have tickled the ghost of Karl Marx.

When stockholders John and Horace Dodge heard
of Ford's plans, they were disturbed. It was true that
they had withdrawn from active participation in the
company and, indeed, had begun the production of a
more expensive car of their own, but they felt that
they had played a vital role in the founding of Ford's
business and were now entitled, morally as well as
legally, to dividends. However, they would be willing, they said, to relinquish their stock if Ford would
buy it; then he could do as he liked. No, Ford replied; he didn't want any more stock. He made the
statement probably unprecedented in the business
world, that the company's profits were too high—
"awful" was the word he used. He would give back
some of this outrageous money to workers and customers but not to himself or any other shareholder. So
the Dodges brought suit for "reasonable" dividends.

The litigation lasted nearly three years. From an
adverse decision in a lower court the case was appealed
in the Supreme Court of Michigan, and early in 1919
Ford was ordered to pay a delayed dividend of $19,-
000,000 with interest at five per cent from the date
of the first decision. It was then that he played what
was probably the most adroit sleight-of-hand performance of his entire career. In the meantime, however, he was involved in circumstances of profound
importance not only to himself but to the nation.

In February 1917, when the tenuous relations with
Germany finally snapped, Ford went into reverse.
With the United States subject to attack, his pacifism
faded out. He offered the services of his factories to the
government. In the time since Sorensen had seen the
assembly line through to triumphant operation at
Highland Park, another Dane of equal talents had
entered Ford's employ. William Knudsen had spent
his first years with Ford reproducing Highland Park
assembly in many branches over the country. He had
become an expert in production short cuts.

Knudsen was faced with his toughest problem
when the Navy asked for the mass production of a
two-hundred-foot submarine chaser called the "Eagle
Boat" and Ford answered with an offer. Six months
after the contract was signed, the first Eagle was
launched; in the next four months forty-three were
built. Although the boats were not a complete success, the fact of their mass production by an automobile plant brought celebrity to the Ford Company.
With the turning out of many ambulances, trucks,
Model T tanks, and Liberty motors, it was usually
admitted that Henry was, after all, a patriot—especially when he said he would rebate to the government
his company's profits on war production. There is no
record of his ever having done this, and it is odd that
so little notice was taken of his failure to do so. But
this, again, was buried in the Ford legend. His assur-
ance that he *intended* to pay back these profits was
enough for the public, and only "carping" critics

have taken him to task for forgetting it. As his most enthusiastic supporters were never given to reading books, they are probably still unaware of the lapse.

By the time the war was over, an enormous new Ford plant at River Rouge in Dearborn was nearing completion. There were large dock facilities, railroad yards, coal and ore bins, blast furnaces, coke ovens, and a foundry thirty acres in area, said to be the largest in the world. The purpose of the plant was the making of steel from ore unloaded at the docks and the fabrication of castings for cylinder blocks, crankshafts, and other things for which Sorensen had produced new methods.

Also, by war's end an old dream had materialized. The idea of using machines to take the drudgery out of farm work had remained in the back of Ford's mind, and now, with plenty of capital at hand, he resumed his boyhood efforts at designing a tractor—this time with an efficient gasoline engine. In order that this activity be immune to attack by stockholders of the Ford Motor Company, he had founded a new concern, Henry Ford and Son, to make the machine. Edsel was made president of this corporation, and the tractor was called the "Fordson." During the war five thousand of them had been mass-produced to help overcome the food shortage in England.

The years of the armistice and peace were checkered for Henry Ford by dark courtroom passages. The agonizing summer days in 1919 fighting the *Tribune's* defense against his libel suit—which he won—were

preceded by his own less embarrassing defense—
which he lost—against the suit of the Dodge brothers
for dividends in 1918. Some of his testimony under
cross-examination in that trial is as revealing of his
mind as any words he ever uttered.

He replied repeatedly that he had all the money he
wanted for himself. Yet he kept repeating the statement that one of the purposes of the Ford Motor Company was to *make money.* The main purpose was
to do good. Yet he would not let that statement stand
alone. It was true, he answered when the Dodges'
lawyer asked him to repeat it, that he wanted to do
good, but he added: "and incidentally to make
money."

But your controlling feature [plaintiff's counsel per-
sisted] since you have got all the money you want, is to
employ a great army of men at high wages, to reduce
the selling price of your car so that a lot of people can
buy it at a cheap price, and give everybody a car that
wants one?
A. If you can give all that, the money will fall into
your hands; you can't get out of it. . . .

Here is the old grass-roots American ethical concept coming out in the characteristically confused answers of a Henry Ford on the witness stand. Making
money is a good in itself. The money is not important;
it is even, sometimes, embarrassing; but the act of
making it is good; *it is inseparably associated with
other good acts.* This conviction laid hold of the Cal-

vinist immigrants as soon as the great wealth the wilderness hid was disclosed; to accumulate a fortune in America meant hard work, which pleased the Calvinist God, but when the reward came the Lord congratulated the worker who had doubled his five talents: "Well done, thou good and faithful servant."

In Ford's little home library, which has been kept intact and is now part of the Ford Archives, there is an annotated volume of Emerson's essays, which (in spite of the "long words" of which he often complained) was part of his favorite reading along with Horatio Alger's stories. In the essay, "Manners," he has marked this passage:

A plentiful fortune is reckoned necessary, in the popular judgment, to the completion of this man of the world. . . .

The rest of the sentence and the context probably baffled Henry Ford, but this much caught his eye, and when the Dodge lawyer questioned him he tried to echo the "popular judgment" as it had been passed on to him in his childhood. "But naturally," he might have said, "you make money! Otherwise the good you do is incomplete!" And, if you do enough good, the money will fall like manna into your lap!

Like most of Ford's courtroom utterances, however damaging they might be within the court, these answers merely confirmed the general conviction that he was a great benefactor, and, as time gives a more and more balanced perspective, history seems to approve this judgment. Whatever his intent, whatever his shortcomings, his ruthlessness, the individual injuries he may have inflicted, the good he did the whole American people must, in any honest appraisal of his era, be conceded to have been immeasurably great.

The Supreme Court handed down its decision in February 1919. It stated that the non-payment of dividends to the stockholders was, considering the remarkable profits, illegal and arbitrary. That it was arbitrary no one could deny, least of all Henry, and, as the court enjoined him from continuing this behavior in the future, he made a resolve never again to allow his arbitrary acts to be subject to any criticism by shareholders. He resolved, in short, to get rid of these encumbrances at the earliest possible moment. But how?

Buy up the minority holdings. For what price? As soon as the stock of Couzens, the Dodges, Anderson, Rackham, and the heirs of John Gray (who had died) was put up for sale Ford was certain to be outbid. Stock of a corporation earning more than sixty million dollars a year was a highly desirable commodity in 1919.

At the moment of the court's decision Ford had already made his first move in anticipation of it. At the end of December 1918 he had resigned from the presidency of his company. He was going, he said, to devote most of his time to tractors and to the publication of a weekly newspaper, the *Dearborn Independ-*

ent. Leaving Edsel in command of the company, he disappeared on a vacation. The next news of him came from Los Angeles, California, and it was startling indeed.

He had dreamed up a new car. It would compete with Model T. It would undersell Model T, going as low as $250. Like Model T, it would be manufactured in Detroit. Giving out a few brief, vague interviews, he trusted to the press and to rumor to build the story up. The game, he knew, must be played adroitly. The story must depress the value of the stock, but it must not kill the sale of Model T. This entailed careful propaganda work among the dealers by Ford's secretary, Ernest Liebold, and by Edsel at Dearborn.

As the potential bidders for Ford stock were scared off by the rumors, secret agents approached the shareholders. They, "now thoroughly frightened," as MacManus tells us, talked it over among themselves, and the conversations seem to have increased their alarm. One by one they sold at the prices offered by the unsuspected buyers—all but Couzens, who smelled a rat. He had, after all, had many opportunities to see Ford in other circumstances that required strategy. He refused to sell until he discovered who was buying. When he did, he raised the ante a thousand dollars a share.

This was all a sleight-of-hand performance more cunning, perhaps, than others in that era of free-and-easy business manipulation. It banked heavily on the

Ford legend. Yet, when it was over, the sold-out stockholders had little to complain of. It left most of them multimillionaires.

On his original investment of less than $2,500 in cash, Couzens received more than $29,000,000. His sister, Mrs. Hauss, who had put in $100 in 1903, got $200,000. Anderson and Rackham made $12,500,000 apiece on $5,000 investments; the Dodges took $25,000,000 between them on $10,-000 (not all of it in cash), and the estate of John Gray, who had bought his shares for $10,500 in cash, came out of it with $10,355,075. All of this was in addition to $30,000,000 in dividends paid to these shareholders over sixteen years!

Ford got what he wanted: total control. A problem remained, however, that he also solved by a trick. Again the trick was made possible by the legend— not, this time, the legend of Henry Ford, but the golden fable of the "ford" with a small letter: the infallible Model T. The payment, all at once, of the sums involved in the stock purchase could not be levied on the company's profits. Even the incredible Ford Motor Company could not suddenly give up seventy-five million in cash and not be dangerously shaken. Yet Ford was determined that the stock should be paid for out of profits and not by banker participation—even though it was necessary to get from the banks a temporary loan pending the arrival of new earnings.

By 1919 his hatred and distrust of bankers had be-

come an obsession. But here there would be no danger of their getting control. With profits at sixty million, the borrowing could be repaid before there could
be any real contamination from the deal. So Ford bor-
rowed his seventy-five million from Old Colony in
Boston and Chase Securities in New York. Then the
depression of 1920 began.

In the last of the war years the price of Model T
had necessarily been raised from $360 in 1917 to
$575 in 1920. Before the depression set in, Ford
had hopefully cut the price from $575 to $440.
Then, in the post-war inflation, he found himself faced
with the danger of selling his car below cost. Even to
the great Ford company a true crisis seemed to be
approaching!

In the emergency he decided to resort to any de-
vice that would prevent his defaulting to the bankers.
Repayment was due in April 1921. The financial
"tour de force," as Keith Sward calls it, that finally
pulled him out was to make Model T pay via the
country-wide network of dealers. He produced some
ninety thousand cars in an operation of fantastic speed
and shipped them to the dealers. The dealers had not
ordered any of these cars, and they threw up their
hands in despair. Take them, Ford advised, or lose
your dealer's franchise. The cars were transported at
the receivers' expense. Cash in payment for the cars
was demanded on delivery.

In panic, the dealers who were not able to pay for

the dumped cars asked their local bankers to finance
them. Thus the burden was transferred to hundreds of
small banks to which Ford was in no wise accountable.
In effect, the small banks were made to pay the big
banks, with the dealers forced to act as unwilling go-
betweens. It was true, of course, that dealers might
refuse, and some did; yet it was a hardy man who
could sacrifice the Ford business on which his reputation and his living had been built, sometimes over
fifteen years.

Like so many near miracles in the life of this dynamic company, this one also worked. In the end,
little Lizzie was responsible. For any lesser car—for
any car, indeed, that had not become as national a tradition as the Conestoga wagon—it is improbable that
the local bankers would have taken a chance. The
number of dealers, however, who suffered heart attacks or hypertension in the process is not on record.

With flying colors, so to speak, Ford came through
on his payments and, as Sward says, "this neat piece
of financing was managed in such a way that it clothed
Wall Street in the dress of Goliath and Ford in the
garb of David." Dealers don't talk—yet to this day, if
one of the old ones is asked in confidence if he remembers 1921, he will have difficulty suppressing
a shudder. Most of them recovered; and, since some
two million cars were produced in the years 1921 and
1922 and, in spite of financial conditions, were all
sold, new fortunes were made all along the line.

In these same years there were some less happy events. One was Henry's sojourn in politics in 1918. He was reluctant to enter Michigan's senatorial race against the candidate of the Republican machine, Truman H. Newberry, but President Wilson wanted him in the Senate.

"I can't leave Detroit," William Adams Simonds quotes him as saying. "I can't take the time to make the race. I've so much to do that I couldn't spend enough time in Washington if I were Senator. Besides, I can't make speeches. . . ."

He was, furthermore, as he said himself, a "born" Republican. Nevertheless, he was in favor of the League of Nations and he had backed Wilson in 1916 with a considerable donation to the Democratic campaign fund because the President had "kept us out of war." Finally, Wilson was grateful for his later war work. The President kept at him until Ford at last threw his hat into the ring.

Once in the fight, he was in it to the finish and, indeed, much further. After a bitter campaign from which the Republicans can hardly be said to have emerged with wholly clean hands, Newberry won the election by a close vote. Ford at once charged a violation of the Corrupt Practices Act, accusing the Republicans of spending an exorbitant campaign fund. He then tried to instigate criminal proceedings on the basis that Newberry had defeated him by fraud, and it is said that he employed detectives to dig up evidence. In time he was able, with assistance from other quarters, to bring about a trial in which Newberry and twelve others involved in the campaign were convicted of violating a Federal statute and sentenced to prison. In 1921 the Supreme Court reversed the decision. Late in 1922, however, as a result of further Ford "persecution," Newberry resigned his seat and, somewhat to Ford's discomfort, his estranged manager James Couzens was appointed to fill Newberry's unexpired term.

The rights and wrongs of the case are too complex for analysis here. Its importance to a Ford biographer is in its revelation of his vindictiveness, once his anger had been aroused. He had been deeply embittered by Republican attacks in the campaign. The Newberry supporters had delivered scathing judgments on his alleged efforts to circumvent Edsel's draft into the armed forces. According to Dean Marquis, Edsel's work at the plant was "absolutely necessary" and "no man . . . rendered a more valuable and patriotic service to his country than he." Nevertheless, the hurt of this public attack went deep. Ford was also portrayed as a "hun-lover" and accused of employing dangerous alien enemies, a maliciously false charge. These things he could not forgive or forget.

Another dark passage during these years was somewhat allied to Ford's participation in politics. This was his publication of the *Dearborn Independent*, which he made into a journal of opinion that enraged large sections of the people. He stood to gain nothing by the violent denunciation of the Jews on the editorial page of this paper, and there has never been any adequate explanation of the attacks. In his reported conversations he often identified Jews and bankers as contemptible people who handled money—a fictional thing that had none of the clean reality of machinery or solid materials. Among other things, the *Independent* printed the Protocols of Zion forgeries, which purported to expose a world-wide conspiracy for Jewish conquest. The anti-Semitic campaign continued for nearly five years, during which the forgery was exposed and Ford was threatened with suit. He then retracted, apologized, and put the entire responsibility on members of the editorial staff who, he maintained, had acted without his knowledge. The patent improbability of this story—especially as the *Independent* contained what was called "Mr. Ford's Own Page," long proclaimed as written by him—has disturbed hero-worshipping biographers ever since, and they have usually evaded the whole subject. Whether or not he composed the bigoted racial diatribes, the fact of their continued appearance remains a permanent stain on his career.

The fact, however, of his having "literary" persons in his employ who could accept this responsibility brings up an important phase that he was entering in the early 1920's. The first editor of the *Dearborn Independent*, E. G. Pipp (who later had some unpleasant things to say about his employer), was replaced by one who remained loyal, William John Cameron. In this time, also, Ford acquired an "aman-

uensis" with a fine flow of language that he was able
to whittle at times into a pretty good imitation of the
way Ford was supposed to think and talk. Samuel
Crowther "collaborated" on three books: *My Life
and Work*, 1922; *Today and Tomorrow*, 1926;
and an astonishing volume called *Moving Forward*
in 1930, which might have been entitled *Requiem
for Model T*.

These gentlemen—and others called in from time
to time—contributed to the popular picture of Ford
a somewhat artificial color. In their writings the simple,
racy language of the master takes on literary clothing.
From the point at which they appear, the beloved
Alger farm-boy mechanic becomes the polished phi-
losopher more appropriate to the mounting millions.
Sometimes he was shown as a profound economist
able to explain with fluid ease and even in professorial
terms some of his industrial successes. In an article in
the *Encyclopædia Britannica* signed "H.F." he becomes the originator of "Mass Production." Here we
find a succession of the "long words" he despised. As
we try to imagine Ford's handsome, serene face and
his gentle voice conjuring such sentences as:

Artificial combination of industrial plants into vast
corporations for financial purposes . . .

or:

However, it was out of the social strife thus engendered that the idea began to emerge that possibly the

difficulty lay in the neglect of scientific manufacturing principles . . .

we wonder what a man who was thrown by the words of the simple Emerson would have made—had he read them—of the tongue-twisters attributed to him by the "amanuenses."

We have been entranced and sometimes awed by the independence of this rugged, iron-willed individualist in the time of his growth. Yet in the years of his middle age we are puzzled by the forms that seem at times to close around him. To be so rich, to be so famous, to be so loved yet so hounded by aggrieved or self-seeking enemies must have made the simple ways, thoughts, and sayings of his youth an impossibility. Too many people were watching, listening, expecting. The rich are wise; they are gentlefolk; they eat off gold plates; they sleep between scented sheets of silk; they are apart; they are educated, tinged by "culture." . . . Can one keep a sure, straight path through such a forest of wealth?

It is certain that Henry Ford repudiated luxury. There is abundant evidence of this in the personal department of the Dearborn museum where the relics that show his habits are preserved. Yet certain necessities arose. A police force was required, for instance, to protect his child and his grandchildren from kidnappers. An army of secretaries and interpreters of all kinds became necessary to his own protection from cranks and crackpots. He becomes, therefore, at a certain point, a little more remote. The biographer finds more and more hurdles between him and his subject. The great no man's land between them is crawling with rumors, hates, vengeances, and envies.

The quoted statements become dubious. Was this or that his real opinion or the inspiration of a ghost writer? It was unfortunate that he was forced—or thought he was forced—to pass the buck of responsibility for the *Independent's* anti-Semitism. After that, how much of what he said might he later deny?

In the meantime, however, over mountain passes and prairies and narrow mesa roads and morasses of mud, Model T rattled on. In 1924 the ten-millionth Ford car moved off the line. In the wake of Lizzie great concrete strips were beginning to unroll. Little hamlets were springing to life, becoming villages, towns, cities. In the wake of Lizzie, trucks began, independent of railroads, to move heavy burdens of freight. Hermit farmers emerged from oblivion, gathered in the centers, entered the social life of larger communities. Roadside markets came into being and truck farms sold their perishable products direct to consumers.

Mass production, brought to its high point in the Ford factories, was applied to other complex luxuries: electric refrigerators, vacuum cleaners, washing machines, radio receiving sets, motion-picture film, phonographs and records. The assembly line had become a new American symbol.

Yet behind all these things, obscured by them, growing, changing, becoming complex too and varying away from formula, stood the common man to whom Henry Ford had devoted so much effort. Was the common man still common? Did he still want things that were ugly, rugged, noisy, but utilitarian? Was he still contemptuous of "the rich" or had he, too, grown rich and full of strange tastes now that his protector, Ford, had so greatly enlarged the whole country's wealth? Had his eyes strayed from his beloved black Lizzie to some painted harlot moving in splendid silence over the smooth paved road?

In the answers to these questions came the first real tragedy Henry Ford had known.

VII

WHAT had happened to the common man before Lizzie's eighteenth year was being demonstrated daily under Henry Ford's nose. Like many men who have grown farsighted from looking over the vast landscape of industrial empire, he failed to see the demonstration. Sometimes, it was thought, he saw it and deplored it, but to accept it as symbolic of what was happening in a world he himself had helped create was beyond his capacity.

The symbol was Edsel. Grandson of a pioneer backwoods farmer, son of a plain man who had begun life with a contempt for luxury, high finance, æsthetics, and book-learning, this boy had been presented on his twenty-first birthday with one million dollars in gold. From that moment it was difficult for the young man to regard only those things that rattled and were painted black as objects of useful value. He became interested in sports, thoroughbred horses, and motor yachts, and—as he was inevitably exposed, in the realms to which these things took him, to "culture"— he acquired taste in the appreciation of the arts. He took seriously, for instance, his appointment to the Detroit art commission, and his gifts to the Detroit Institute of Arts show a selective self-education in a field remote from his father's ken. It became natural, then,

as he matured, for his eyes to follow a car with a handsome body, quiet motor, and smooth transmission and,
when little black Lizzie came bouncing along the
street with puffs, coughs, and backfires, to turn his
attention to something his milieu had taught him was
prettier.

Edsel was, of course, an extreme case. But all over
the country, sons of the very men and women to
whom Henry Ford had brought prosperity were going through a similar smoothing of the parental rug-
gedness. No one knew or will ever know how many
boys the Model T sent to college. It and a hundred
mass-produced work-savers that had followed in its
train had softened and refined the whole of life. The
American boy or girl coming to maturity in the middle twenties rarely received a million dollars as a
birthday gift, but many of them got enough to make
them quite different from their fathers, enough to incline them to regard with embarrassment their parents'
callused hands, weathered faces, and black, consump-
tive cars.

Apparently, then, mass production—at least on the
Ford pattern—created wealth, but wealth did not
reply in kind: the consumer's wealth made it increasingly difficult for rigid mass production to function.
It seems, then, as if both Model T and the assembly
line contained the germs of their own destruction:
they brought prosperity, and prosperity repudiated
standardization! The assembly line has not, of course,
been destroyed; only its economic value has suffered;

and this may be restored when this great American technique becomes more flexible.

Before the debacle Edsel's interest in design—in "styling"—caused disagreement between father and son. It has been said that Henry fired one of his executives for "putting" such ideas into Edsel's mind. But no one put these ideas in the young man's mind, he simply acquired them and liked them. His work with the expensive Lincoln car, which the Ford company had taken over from the Lelands in 1922, had given him experience.

Edsel had a mind of his own, though it was characteristic of his father not to think so.

Edsel Ford [wrote William C. Richards in his fascinating assembly of Fordiana, *The Last Billionaire*] was a personality in his own right but he was more or less overlooked and submerged because his father was a more electric and involved study.

Yet, however strong Edsel might have been, he could never have convinced his father that Madame T had outlived her time. Executives, salesmen, engineers, trade journals, gossip, such echoes of public opinion as came to his ears—none of these could divert him from the total dedication to an idea that had arrived with the first design of the little car. His ear, for example, failed to catch the first really sour notes of the jokes:

Why is a Ford like a bathtub? Because you hate to be seen in one.

Only one argument entered and disturbed the loneliness of his night thoughts. This was statistics. Behind the statistics was a creature of William Knudsen's imagination, evolved after Knudsen had left the Ford Motor Company. It has been thought that letting Knudsen go was Ford's greatest mistake, although someone, later, would surely have dreamed Knudsen's dream. At General Motors he conjured up something much prettier, with a more sophisticated name and not much more expensive than Lizzie.

By her close friends—who were legion soon after her appearance—Bill Knudsen's girl was called Chevvy.

In 1923 the Model T production was 1,699,984. General Motors was the closest competitor, with 798,555 total production of all cars. Chevrolet was G.M.'s best seller—464,800. In 1924, called a "recession" year, Ford sales dropped only about 15 per cent, to a 28 per cent setback for Chevrolet. The future, therefore, looked rosy enough for Model T. Then, with 1925, came a boom, the beginning of the meteoric climb to the spectacular crash of '29. To the consternation of the Ford watchers—except Henry —Model T did not respond to the general stimulus. It even fell back—only about sixty thousand to be sure, yet in the same year Knudsen's car regained all she had lost and a little more. This "handwriting on the wall" seems faint enough. Yet the hardheaded businessmen at Ford were deeply disturbed. Henry, for all his cleverness at big deals, was not in the "hard-headed" tradition. He was a man of faith, a bold adventurer—in many ways a true romantic. What, he asked, were these men talking about, with the beloved flivver selling more than a million and a half a year in the United States alone? They tried to explain that things were changing. They said that in 1925, when everything else had turned to the up and up, Ford profits had declined by twenty million dollars. But Henry was not interested in what his competitors were doing: he was doing so much himself, he could not take the time to attend to these remote omens.

And he was, indeed, doing more than any ten ordinary industrialists could well attend to! He had already started the building of his "empire." He could no longer expand very far within the framework of the automobile business itself, and yet mounting profits had constantly lured him toward expansion. He therefore looked to see how far he could trace back his materials to their sources and then control the sources. So he bought up all kinds of properties and engaged in various expensive experiments with things that at first seemed to have faint connection with little Lizzie.

He bought a railroad. It was a small affair called Detroit, Toledo and Ironton, but Henry made it into a big one, increased its profits, and used it for his own extensive shipments, thereby saving considerable freight costs. He acquired the control of sixteen coal mines, about seven hundred thousand acres of timberland in Michigan and Kentucky, built a sawmill that

cut three hundred thousand feet of timber a day,
built a fleet of Great Lakes steamers 612 feet long to
bring ore from the Superior deposits direct to River
Rouge, bought a glass works, vast tracts of land for
the growing of soybeans and flax, dug a canal, and
made many arrangements to facilitate communications
among sixty American, nine Canadian, and twenty
foreign plants or branches of the Ford Motor Company.

This was what economists call a "vertical" trust—
controlling materials from their raw state to final fabrication. Along with this, Ford and his associates were
working out what later became celebrated as the
"moving inventory." His aim was to have no ware-
houses, to store nothing, but to keep every scrap of
material constantly in transit or in motion through
machinery. Thus only just enough ore arrived at River
Rouge for the blast furnaces to handle each day; only
enough lumber for the floor boards in a single day's
production of cars came into the plant in the course of
twenty-four hours, and so on. The ideal was to have
Ford materials in various stages of completion moving
all over the world in ships and trains. The scheme, of
course, required a miracle of timing and continuous
work on schedules.

Apart from all this, there was much experiment
with innovation that might or might not have future
uses: soybean plastics, new machine-processing of
flax for linen for tops and artificial leather, a continuous plate-glass process for windshields (which actu-

ally antedated the celebrated Pittsburgh process), and the development of all sorts of small rural industries, according to Henry's theory of "decentralization." In somewhat that same category came the scheme to assemble cars not merely at the central plant but at some place near the selling point—hence the division between manufacturing and assembly plants that saved so much difficult transportation. It is easier—and far more in the mass-production pattern—to ship parts than finished cars. Then there were the economy processes, the salvaging of floor sweepings—scrap paper and metal—and smoke control and a dozen other methods of saving with which Ford was forever experimenting.

Finally there were the manufacture of airplanes and the beginnings of the strange historical hobby. All these things filled the spaces left in Henry's mind by the extremely smooth production of a car that had changed very little in seventeen years. Other motor-makers were busy thinking about each year's new car models, their special features of design and "sales appeal." For Ford there was none of this, for Model T was eternal. Yet it was a happy thing for Henry that when the time came when his beloved creation would be no more—when his interest in automobiles would seem to fade away—there were so many things to take its place in his indomitably active mind.

The crisis from which no sane man could turn away arrived in 1926. In that year Ford production dropped by more than a quarter million, General Motors sales came within a few thousand of Ford production, G.M. could claim about 28 per cent of total United States output, and little Chevvy had jumped to over 600,000. As E. D. Kennedy writes in his *The Automobile Industry*:

The American public was still buying about twice as many Fords as Chevrolets—but it had bought about six times as many as recently as 1924. And, comparisons aside, Ford's own production record showed a decline of more than 300,000 cars in the past twelve months.

In 1926 Chevrolet's coupé price was $645, whereas Ford's had got down to the all-time low of $290. But Model T at that price was stripped bare of such things as a self-starter and demountable rims, which were standard equipment in Chevvy. For not very much more, then, you could buy a really "smart" little car with many advantages that had come both through increased research and invention and because the functions a car must perform had changed. The planetary gears, for instance, which had pulled Lizzie out of many a critical spot, were no longer needed on hard, smooth roads, and were a drawback when speed was desired. Also, this gear system had a peculiar effect described by Lee Stout White in his classic, *Farewell to Model T*:

Even if the car was in a state known as neutral, it trembled with a deep imperative and tended to inch forward.

Cooling systems, magnetos, shock-absorbers, and lamps were superior on other cars. In 1926, if you could dig up the price of a fully equipped Ford, you could usually manage somehow to get, say, twenty-five per cent more and splurge on a job you could be proud of. But by 1926 an even more sinister and destructive termite had begun to gnaw at the industry. To most manufacturers in that high, wide, and handsome decade there had been no thought of a possible saturation point—a point at which every man, woman, and mewling infant would own a car and no more would be wanted. Or if this was considered as a threat, it was evaded by putting over on the public the extraordinary hoax that it was more economical to turn in your old car and get a new one every few years than to cling to what you had. This was good for the industry, but what about the car you turned in?

Used cars were as much of a threat to Ford as was Chevrolet. For less than the price of a new Model T you could buy, in 1926, an elderly Buick, for example, and, for the difference, have its face lifted. Old as it might be, it would have features that Lizzie, designed in 1908 and never basically altered, still lacked!

Gently, tactfully, but with the insistence of buzzing mosquitoes, the alarmed executives at Highland Park kept telling these things to sixty-three-year-old Henry Ford. It was an attack on his whole philosophy. For eighteen years he had preached, talked to reporters, dictated books and magazine articles on the

"Messiah" of his kind of mass production come to save the world. For this philosophy he was celebrated in every corner of the globe in which there was a single economist. It had been translated into many languages; it had a European name: "Fordismus." It had become the essence—the life blood, almost—of Henry Ford's being.

It is said that he fired some of the talkers, that he kept walking out of the room while they argued, that he quibbled over every detail of change they advocated. He clung to his statement that "the only trouble with the Ford car is that we can't make them fast enough." He accused his rivals of backing their prospects "into a corner and selling them," forgetting that his own dealers were accomplished in this technique, and he railed at installment-selling, in which his dealers were also engaged. In many ways in this transition he behaved like a stubborn and crotchety old man, yet it is impossible not to feel the poignancy of his dilemma. For he had worked real miracles.

Fifteen million of his little car had been sold— about four fifths of these in the United States—so it could be said statistically that one American out of ten had owned a new Ford. Its production on this scale had been possible *only* because it had remained unchanged. Its sales had produced seven billion dollars, gross. As Keith Sward said, it had brought into being:

the most advanced technological apparatus yet conceived since the dawn of the Industrial Revolution. During its youth and in its prime, the Model T was indeed the wonder child of the magic city of mass production, a gigantic social force.

We do not know about the intimate moments of this tragedy's consummation. The Ford-can-do-no-wrong writers have left out this most moving of all performances, pretending that their immaculate subject was, after all, a sensible fellow once he saw the facts and, indeed, jumped to the decision that a change was needed. This is the position he is made to take in the book "collaborated in" by Samuel Crowther, *Moving Forward*, a shocking betrayal of all Ford's vital convictions.

It has been supposed [says this book, for example] that our company was an exponent of mass production. This has never been true.

Whether or not Ford in some exasperated moment actually said this thing, there is little excuse for its embodiment in print. It and many other statements in this apologia must have hurt Henry Ford's reputation for integrity as much as any of the stories told by his bitterest enemies.

In the last months of the summer of 1926 Lizzie was sent to a beauty parlor in some desperate last-minute experiments. She was swung lower. Her impudent little snub nose, which had turned up at so many sandy hills or pools of slime, was smoothed out. Finally—most radical of all, considering her maker's early Yankee witticism about "any color so long as it's black"—she appeared, as Sward says, like "a renovated ancient dowager on her last fling . . . in fawn gray, gunmetal blue, phoenix brown and highland green."

It did no good. Perhaps it was a sop to Henry: it must have been vinegar indeed on his tongue. Lizzie's production was discontinued in May 1927, and the Highland Park plant shut down. The repercussions were felt throughout industrial and business America. Some sixty thousand Detroit workers were said to have been laid off. Remote places were affected by the waves from this stone dropped into the industrial pool. When it is remembered that at this time the automotive industry used 18 per cent of the national supply of iron and steel, 74 per cent of the plate glass, 85 per cent of the rubber, 60 per cent of the upholstery leather, 28 per cent of the nickel, 27.7 per cent of the aluminum, 24.1 per cent of the tin, 14.6 per cent of the copper, and 18.8 per cent of the hardwood, it is evident that the closing down of a plant which had turned out more than 50 per cent of the nation's automobiles was a serious shock even in the boom year of 1927.

It was soon realized, of course, that, though Lizzie's funeral was in full progress, there was nothing dead about the Ford Motor Company. The company's net worth as of December 31, 1926, was $714,902,-288. This was twenty-five per cent of the total net worth of all motor companies. In 1925 the *New York Times* reported that the Ford family had re-

ceived personal dividends, over and above salaries, of
nearly fifteen millions. It was simply a question of
building a new, completely retooled plant at River
Rouge in Dearborn. Ford always did things in a clean
sweep. Once the decision came to make a new car,
there was no compromise.

And Model A, as the new car was called, was no
compromise either. It was a new job from radiator to
rear axle. It had standard transmission, four-wheel
brakes, hydraulic shock-absorbers, windshield wiper,
and a safety-glass windshield. Finally, to the real aston-
ishment of the trade, Model A sold for very little more
than Lizzie and still undersold Chevvy by about a
hundred dollars!

Having surrendered thus far, however, Henry still
clung to his opposition to a yearly change of model.
On its first appearance, the Model A was immensely
popular. Loyal Ford owners were delighted to be able
to drive something that, though still a Ford, would
not be laughed at. In the five years, however, during
which Henry refused to change A, it too became obso-
lescent and there was heavy competition not only from
Chevrolet but from Walter Chrysler's Plymouth. The
V-8 appeared in 1932. This was one of Ford's tri-
umphs over the persuasions of his subordinates. They
had been bringing pressure for a six-cylinder car. One
of his most cantankerous arguments had been about
the "unbalance" of a six-cylinder engine. He jumped,
therefore, from four to eight, and it was not until 1936
that he was persuaded, not by his engineers but by

his dealers, to try a six in competition with other low-priced cars.

As Ford's company came to conform to prevailing trends with Model A, it seemed to lose some of its independence, its individuality, its fierce scorn of imitation. Between A and V-8, for instance, the company followed the lead of General Motors in establishing a subsidiary corporation to finance time payments. Through dealer complaints, Ford, G.M., and Chrysler all came under the scrutiny of the Department of Justice for this and similar practices, and all three were eventually indicted for so-called violation of the Sherman Anti-Trust Act and would have been prosecuted but for the promise of good behavior. Such things were, perhaps, of no great importance to the life of a company, though conformity to trends—as in the later case of the labor unions—showed a departure from early standards that may have been due to the inevitable pressure of the times or that may have been indications of a slight weakening of an aging man's grip on the enormous machine.

Throughout Ford's life there are recurrent demonstrations of his personal power, yet as he grew older his energies and enthusiasms were spread over an ever widening field. A man cannot well be a museum director, an antique collector, a researcher in history, an educator, a promoter of aviation, a farmer, a health authority, a developer of hydroelectric power, a master of square dancing—all of which Ford was, and a political dabbler as well—and keep his full concentration on the manufacture of automobiles. As these activities were, however, important to Henry's private life, they must be explored in any attempt to evolve a complete portrait.

In 1922 he listened for a while to a Ford-for-President agitation. That such a movement should start is not surprising. Americans who become sufficiently celebrated for any reason—especially if they are popular and regarded as public benefactors—usually encounter this suggestion, and it is a hardy man who repudiates the flattery. Ford went so far as to publish an article in *Collier's* in the summer of 1923 entitled "If I Were President." In an opinion poll he was a thirty-per-cent choice for the Democratic nomination. His special appeal was economic as well as personal. As Preston Slosson wrote in *The Great Crusade and After*:

This great popularity rested in part on the Ford policy of reducing costs to the consumer and raising wages to the worker out of his own profits . . . but in part it must be explained by the pleasant personality of Henry Ford himself. . . . He had the democratic geniality and "folksiness" which Michigan and her neighbor states ranked as chief of human virtues.

The facts, however, that, by his own avowal, reading was difficult for him, books "mussed up his mind," he could not make speeches, his interest in political history was nil, and he avoided personal public ap-

pearances, especially if he was expected to be articulate, alarmed many people who might otherwise have
favored his nomination. His closer admirers and well-
wishers feared the ridicule and humiliation that would
attend these weaknesses when revealed to a president's
merciless critics. They were greatly relieved, therefore,
when, after a talk with President Coolidge, then filling
Harding's unexpired term, he withdrew and declared
that he would favor the nomination of this even less
articulate Republican.

Details of the conference with Coolidge were not
given out, but it was thought that the close-lipped Ver-
monter had won Ford's support by favoring private
ownership of the Muscle Shoals project—one of
Ford's pets on which he had made a bid. Ford was
deeply interested in hydroelectric development and
saw great possibilities in carrying on the operations on
the Tennessee River begun by President Wilson for
wartime production of nitrates. This was an even more
urgent dream than that of the presidency, and Ford
may well have thought that under the continuing
favor of Coolidge it might be fulfilled.

Private ownership of this gigantic power plan was,
however, so strongly and cogently opposed by Ne-
braska's Senator George Norris that even Coolidge
and his Republican Congress were never able to put
it through. Norris began his fifteen-year fight (which
ended with the establishment of the Tennessee Valley
Authority under Franklin Roosevelt) with a violent
attack on the Ford offer, in which he was joined by

Arthur Vandenberg and James Couzens, both of
Michigan. By the end of 1924 Ford knew he was
beaten. "We must have lost our interest," he announced, "in Muscle Shoals. Productive business cannot wait on politics."

In that year he had become increasingly interested
in aviation. Here he played an important pioneering
part. A brilliant aircraft designer, William Bushnell
Stout, who had been unsuccessful with a Navy plane,
came to Detroit with the stubborn determination to
interest automobile manufacturers in an all-metal mon-
oplane. He interested Edsel Ford. Shortly afterward
an announcement gave the news of a new Ford activity:

For the purpose of encouraging aircraft development,
the Ford interests are erecting near the Dearborn laboratory a modern factory building and hangar which will
be devoted to research work in aviation. A landing
field nearly three quarters of a mile square is being
leveled. . . .

Here the *Maiden Dearborn,* an all-metal Stout
plane with a Ford Liberty motor as power plant, was
built and proved so successful that Ford bought Stout's
company and produced the trimotored Ford airplane
known as the "Tin Goose." From the Ford airport in
April 1925 operations began on the first commercial
airline with regularly scheduled flights in the United
States. There were daily flights to Chicago and back
and to Cleveland and back, totaling nearly eight hun-

dred miles at an average speed of between ninety and a hundred miles an hour. Henry's justifiably proud boast was that in the first year of operation there was not a single accident or a day's interruption of service —a record American feat in 1925.

At the Ford airport, as Christy Borth tells us in his *Masters of Mass Production*, "the pioneering was done on those radio beams that have now become standard skyway markers all over the world." U.S. Patent No. 1,937,876, for which the Ford Motor Company applied in May 1928, described "a radio beacon . . . which will send out a signal in a predetermined direction so that a pilot may fly on the signal and may be kept upon its course by following the signal." The Ford-Stout operations were a significant prelude to the extensive part Ford was to play in aircraft manufacture in World War II.

On the lighter side of the vast ledger recording Ford enthusiasms stood one that Henry himself took very seriously. This was the square dance. His passion for gavottes, schottisches, quadrilles, and Virginia reels apparently had its inception in one of those intervals of nostalgia that often occurred on a relaxed evening. Conversation at a party of old friends turned upon the kind of dance that had enhanced Henry's courtship of Clara in Springwells Township back in the eighties. According to Richards, who has given us by far the most intimate and colorful account of this phase of Ford's life, the guests played a kind of game, trying to remember the "calls" and the steps of the dances, and finally Clara said:

"Do you realize, Henry Ford, that we have danced very little since we were married? . . . It would do us both good to take it up again."

Richards shows the wonderful way in which such a casual seed, which with most other couples would be soon forgotten, could come to blossom with the Fords:

The idyll of long ago is usually lost for good; the pressed flower in the book remains powder, but Ford had a commingling of zeal and wealth that was a magic restorative. The idyll could be made to throb again, the perfume of the flower recaptured.

Beginning with a barn dance on Halloween in 1924, the preoccupation lasted nearly twenty years and consumed quantities of time and money. A dance instructor, Benjamin Lovett, was put on Ford's payroll and came with his wife to live at Dearborn. An orchestra was kept in permanent attendance, ready on call, day or night, in business hours or on holidays, to assemble and play. A ballroom was constructed in the engineering laboratory in which special flooring was laid. It was separated by canvas from a drafting room.

Men bent over blueprints of a dirigible a few yards from where the orchestra played *Pop Goes the Weasel*.

Eventually this "ballroom" was replaced by Lovett Hall, named after the teacher:

. . . paneled chastely, floored with costly teakwood, furnished in English colonial and reached by winding marble. . . .

One of Ford's ideas was that the old square dances were a means of reviving old-fashioned formal courtesy: amenities that had been destroyed by the fox trots, bunny hugs, and hip-flask accompaniments of the 1920's. In an effort to convince the young of this, a dancing class of adolescents was instituted at Dearborn.

The dancing fanaticism of Henry revealed an extraordinary combination of autocracy and gentleness. The dance itself to him was a demonstration of the "graciousness" and simple boy-and-girl relations of a pioneer American period. He made it, however, a discipline for his subordinates. Invitations to his top executives to bring their wives to a Ford dance were commands. Sometimes he would call them out of their offices in the middle of a morning to learn a new step. Everywhere in and around Detroit a Ford dance invitation was an excuse to call off any other social event.

It was in his dancing phase that Henry departed from some of the simpler tenets of his early life. Although it was presumably a relic of harvest nights in cold barns, it became embellished by Ford wealth. His dancing shoes were made by a cobbler retained for the purpose. His invitations finally went out to the rich and great of Grosse Pointe—people he had once despised. The orchestra and other features belonged more in the category of the king's jester and the sultan's harem than most American extravagances.

It was, of course, good copy for the press. Like everything else he did—his before-breakfast sprints at sixty, his fence-jumping, his vaulting, his handsprings, his practical jokes, his genial, primitive humor —Henry's dancing was a subject of endless public comment. Yet it began a healthy interest in an almost forgotten American tradition. Along with the revival of the barn dance came new interest in folk music, ballads, songs that under the ceaseless clangor of the machine sequence had faded out.

Was it, indeed, true that this titan of mass production wanted, in his relaxed moments, to find some balance for the dehumanizing forces he had let loose upon the world?

VIII

"THE ROUGE is so big," Henry Ford said to a *Fortune* writer in 1933, "that it is no fun any more."

He had moved his private office to a place where there was more fun. This was the Engineering Laboratory in Dearborn, four miles from the plant. Adjacent were Henry's two pet projects: the museum in which he pursued his own peculiar variety of history, and the beloved Greenfield Village, where the strange assortment of sentimental monuments had been accumulating ever since the death of Model T. Now the village had a school in full operation where the children were taught as Ford believed children should be taught in a replica of the building in which he had achieved his own sketchy education. Here he was patron saint: he would sit listening to the singing or watching the dancing that were studied along with McGuffey *Readers*, and the children would come forward to greet him—shy and awed at first, then enticed out of themselves by a charm he reserved for the very young.

In the post-Model T years Ford had turned also to vaster hobbies. He owned tracts of farm land through "down-state" Michigan that were almost unbelievable in size. Between seven and eight thousand acres were devoted to the cultivation of soybeans. Ford was an enthusiast for chemurgy, the industrial use of agricultural products. His experiments with plastics and fiber made from soybeans were said to be costly and the whole project was given up by Henry II, but in the mid-1930's a bushel of soya went into every Ford car. In Ways, Georgia, where his plantation extended over eighty-five thousand acres, his experiments with lettuce, sweet potatoes, and sugar cane were pure hobby, as was his wild-game sanctuary. Here he exercised a benevolent fatherly overlordship. According to *Time*:

> His neighbors are Georgia Crackers whom he permits to dwell on his acres under a kind of feudal patronage. They are allowed to work in the sawmill, the general store, the nursery. There are garden plots for families, schools for children.

Another idea was what he described as "turning back to village industry." This grew into a large decentralization blueprint, never fully developed. The theory, as Crowther elucidated it, was not unique with Henry: it has been under serious consideration for many years by industrial planners. With Henry, it may have sprung from the observation that the Rouge was too big.

> Therefore, to get rid of the overhead of the big city, to try to find the balance between industry and agriculture, and more widely to distribute the purchasing power of the wages we pay among the people who buy our products we began to decentralize.

Ford and Crowther wrote this in 1926 when his executives were daily taking Model T's temperature and shaking their heads. He began with an old mill at Northville up the River Rouge, which he turned into a valve shop. He staffed it with his mechanics, whom he then tried to interest in rural occupations.

We have not drawn men from the farms—we have added industry to farming. One worker operates a farm which requires him to have two trucks, a tractor and a small closed car. Another man, with the aid of his wife, clears more than five hundred dollars a season on flowers. We give any man a leave of absence to work on his farm, but with the aid of machinery these farmers are out of the shops a surprisingly short while. . . .

Here is the boyhood conviction again! Take the drudgery out of farming and it becomes, not a full-time slavery, but an adjunct to an abundant life.

After Northville, Waterford, Phoenix, and Plymouth on the Rouge began making small things for the factory or the car, plants with hydroelectric power were put to work on the Huron River, at Hamilton, Ohio, and at Green Island on the Hudson. One as far west as Los Angeles was set to making fabric of Imperial Valley cotton.

These experiments came in for a good deal of fun-making by the eager critics, and it is true that they did not fulfill their economic purpose. Such an implacable enemy as Keith Sward says that they served mainly as

publicity material "for the sermonettes fashioned by
W. J. Cameron for the Ford Sunday Evening Hour."
It seems unlikely that such extensive effort should have
been designed for these purposes. The scheme did
not work, no doubt: so revolutionary a plan can
hardly be put into operation so quickly and with the
accompaniment of the period's national upheaval and
be wholly successful. Yet as a full-scale model of
something which may evolve—under the pressure of
air war if at no other instance—can we say the thing
was of no value? May not an experimenter on Ford's
scale—with endless resources and little concern over
lost expense—do something for our future that no one
else can do? Are there not too few Fords, recklessly
driving into unknown and dangerous fields to prove
a conviction?

A hardheaded grandson, Henry Ford II, has sold
the soybeans and the Ford "fleet," but is still concerned with decentralization.

I sincerely believe [the *Atlantic Monthly* quotes
Henry Ford II as saying in the year of his father's death]
that our heavy concentration in the Rouge plant makes
our organization job and all phases of our human relations job more difficult. . . .

I do not mean . . . that we are planning any large-
scale moves in a hurry. . . . But I do think that over
a period of time our company and most of the people in
it will be better off if our extreme concentration in the
Rouge is reduced.

He may well study the working model to which his grandfather gave so much thought and tried with the characteristic haste in which he moved toward so many of his ideals to make into an overnight reality.

It might well be supposed from the apparent flight from "bigness," the change in his headquarters, the indulgence in a score of activities only remotely if at all concerned with the manufacture of automobiles, that Ford, at seventy, had partly retired. Yet no guess could be more false. With all the various movement in what has been called his "twenty-track mind," he never relaxed his dictator's grip on the company. His physical presence at the Rouge had lessened. Yet every lieutenant reflected his mood: his will was transmitted from the lowest foreman to the lowest sweeper. Mr. Ford says, Mr. Ford thinks, Mr. Ford wants, Mr. Ford has ordered, Mr. Ford has forbidden— these words echoed in every corridor; they were spoken in the cabins of the giant traveling cranes, in the hiatuses between the drops of an eight-hundred-ton punch press.

The top executives came almost daily to a luncheon at Ford's office. The meal would last, sometimes, five hours. They would eat, off a round table, simple American food served by colored waiters. They would bring up such problems as they dared. Certain subjects became taboo. A constant worry to the business administrators in the heavy depression years (1931– 33) came from the great losses, totaling some $150,-

000,000, and the fact that Chevrolet for three suc-
cessive years was selling more than Model A. One
day, according to *Fortune*, Henry put a stop to it.

"I guess," he said, "the Chevrolet people have accomplished what they set out to do all right . . . to
get you fellows' minds off your work."

"I don't know [he told the *Fortune* writer] how many
cars Chevrolet sold last year. I don't know how many
they may sell next year. And—I don't care."

It was characteristic of him to brush off these matters that so disturbed men who were constantly exposed, in those days, to the constant ugly rumors of
the depression. Experience had made him so confident
that sums in nine figures, whether they were losses or
gains, no longer impressed him. Market fluctuations
were an old story. He refused to be depressed by the
depression. Again and again between 1929 and 1934
he gave out statements that shocked those who had
watched the agony in the bread lines. He said the
depression was "wholesome," that people would
profit by the "illness" because "the recovery is pro-
longed"; that "these are the best times we ever had."
How he reconciled these beliefs with the conditions
he must have seen about him puzzled some observers,
especially when in 1932 a "hunger march" on the
Rouge ended in a riot in which four paraders were
killed.

Aloof as Henry Ford may have been, however,
from a world in which financial disaster and Chevro-

let sales were all part of the same chaos, he kept in-
formed about what went on within the Ford Motor
Company. He continued to solidify his control by his
celebrated "purges." It has never been understood
why he had fired, or made their jobs intolerable for,
some of the very men who had built his success, because he struck, always, with an intuitive mind. He
skipped the intermediate rational steps most of us go
through. He could not, therefore, give his reasons.
Sometimes he would pass the buck to Sorensen. But
what mystified observers still more was that the departure of these seemingly indispensable men made
no apparent difference to the success of the company.
Key engineers, administrators, public-relations experts—Couzens, Knudsen, Marquis, Klingensmith,
Pipp, Hawkins, Wills, and many others—had somehow come to a parting of the ways with Henry. The
days even of Liebold and the great Sorensen were
numbered.

There was one man, however, whom he never
fired. There was one man whose power became almost
as great as Henry's, who was still in his saddle when
Henry was through. It was from him that Ford got
most of his information about the inside of Rouge,
big as it was, for nearly twenty years. And it was this
man who was at the point of the wedge when the
Rouge met its long-delayed labor crisis in the last
years before the Second World War. His name was
Harry Herbert Bennett, and in its later phases he had
no rival anywhere in the Ford shop.

A fiction-writer would be hard put to devise a more dramatic, picaresque, ingenious, or imaginative character. Surely in the later history of industry he is without a peer. There were grimmer personalities in Homestead, in Beaver County steel, in West Virginia coal, and other settings of key labor conflicts, but none so colorful: none more alternately charming and ruthless; none whose devices were more fanciful and devious. And he made no bones about his attributes. Once when he was given a manuscript biography of himself by an admiring writer he handed it back.

"No one," he said, "will recognize me."

"But why?"

"You don't say I'm a son of a bitch."

William Richards, who tells this story, also describes some of the five estates that, during his career with Ford, Bennett acquired. In one "castle" to which he repaired in times of stress a secret door led from a bathroom to a tunnel forty feet long ending in the garage. Thus, whatever forces of justice or retribution he might fancy were after him, Harry Bennett could retire and be a hundred miles away by the time his pursuer began to wonder what kept him so long. In a room of his Grosse Ile house in which he entertained:

picking up a bottle no different from a dozen others, released a spring, the private bar swung open . . . and behind it steps led to the boat well of his 70-foot, all steel yacht.

On duty, Harry Bennett was a policeman—or, rather, a chief of police. This was covered by the euphemistic title "Director of Personnel." It was true that hiring and firing came within his purview, as well as the screening of applicants for jobs and the various strong-arm methods of enforcing discipline not uncommon in large industrial plants before they were unionized. For these purposes he had built up what was often referred to as a "gestapo" or "G.P.U."—an effective army of boxers, football players, ex-detectives, and men handy with heavy makeshift weapons.

A former sailor and boxing champion himself, Bennett had drifted into the Rouge during the dangerous days of World War I when the enormous influx of war workers could not be handled with gloves. Only five and a half feet tall, he had attracted attention by laying out some recalcitrant workers twice his size: he was made supervisor and soon came to Henry Ford's attention. Ford gave him an appropriate office in a basement, from which he directed operations that in time were said to cover vast tracts and dark corners of Detroit's underworld.

As the Ford grandchildren came along, Bennett furnished a guard to keep potential kidnappers away. The poor children must often have been harassed by these watchers in the bushes, but it was one of Ford's dominant and reasonable fears that a child would be held for the fabulous ransom he could give. It was said that Bennett, by his acquaintance with criminals of all stripes, was able to obtain information and thwart conspiracies that could not have been stopped in any other way. In any case, it is well known that he took in some notorious convicts, such as Chester Le Mare on parole, giving them employment on his force. Bennett had no hesitation in admitting this: he was showing the men, he said, "how to go straight."

Bennett's force was dignified by the name of Ford Service Department. It was this organized company police force that, more than any other discomforts, irked the workers and proved the best selling point for the organizers of the C.I.O. It furnished opportunity for those tales of abuse and bloodshed that labor organizations relish and that have often formed for them an opening wedge. Unfortunately, in the case of the Rouge, some of the stories were true.

By spring of 1937 the United Auto Workers of the C.I.O. had called strikes in General Motors and Chrysler and had secured contracts. In the ranks of U.A.W., "Ford next" was a familiar slogan. The most eager agitators, however, were aware of the difficulties. The Rouge was called by labor's champion, Mary Heaton Vorse, "the most impregnable citadel of the employers."

The River Rouge plant [she wrote] is like a bastille. Ford is as independent of detective agencies and strike-breaking organizations as he is of banks. He has his own strong arm men. . . .

And Ford, moreover, had sworn eternal resistance to organization. "We will never recognize," he said, "the United Auto Workers' Union or any other union. Labor union organizations are the worst thing that ever struck the earth because they take away a man's independence." His reasons for this antagonism were remarkable. He believed that unions were products of Wall Street; that bankers had instigated them to trap the workers!

There is no mystery [he told his men] about the connection between corporation control and labor control. They are the two ends of the same rope. A little group of those who control both capital and labor will sit down in New York and settle prices, dividends—and wages.

When the National Labor Relations Act was passed in 1935 he said:

The Ford Motor Company has had a labor relations act for years. I would be ashamed to have anyone tell me our conditions and pay are wrong. That part of my job was started twenty years ago. I have heard no complaints from our men. There is nothing a union can give them that they haven't already got. I haven't given the Wagner Act a thought. We've always had it in force.

Since then he had consistently refused to respect any of the labor legislation that had come in with the New Deal. This defiant attitude, quite unusual by 1937 among large employers, made an approach to Ford's "bastille" peculiarly difficult for the U.A.W., especially when the gigantic shadow of that tough little fighter, Bennett, lay across the entrance.

In May, however, the union was heartened by at least one portent. The city of Dearborn had, perhaps because of the new legislation, agreed to give union organizers permits to stand outside the Rouge gates and distribute leaflets as the shifts changed and the workers came out. This and the legal right to solicit membership in the union emboldened them to make their peaceful march. On the twenty-sixth, then, having given plenty of advance notice, the U.A.W.'s representatives (sixty per cent women) went to the gates at shift-changing time. What ensued is still celebrated in labor history as the "Battle of the Overpass."

The bridge in question led over Miller Road to Gate No. 4 of the Rouge. The company had built it so as not to snarl up traffic on the street when the shifts came out. It had, however, had plenty of public use. Venders, selling to the workers, were in the habit of taking their stand here. Two officials of the union, Walter Reuther and Richard Frankensteen, not supposing—or so they said—that the overpass was restricted to Ford labor, attempted to use it as an observation post from which to survey the proceedings. They were accompanied by a minister, the Reverend Raymond P. Sandford, who later gave his eyewitness account at an N.L.R.B. hearing. A group of "servicemen" standing on the overpass ordered them off and then, before they could comply, gave Reuther and

Frankensteen the kind of brutal beating that, when it was described in its shocking detail in the Labor Board's report, was certain to win public sympathy for the union. In other places, four other union men received the same rough treatment at the hands of Harry Bennett's guard.

The whole affair might well have been softened in the press or turned in favor of management, as most newspapers at the time opposed the growing power of the C.I.O. Bennett's boys, however, made one tactical error—not surprising, perhaps, as such men are rarely noted for discretion. They attacked the reporters and news photographers, tore up films, and exposed plates. These things were not forgotten when the news stories were written.

When the Battle of the Overpass was reviewed by the National Labor Relations Board, the Ford Company was ordered to "cease and desist" discouraging union membership, maintaining "vigilante or similar groups; or using its service department for intimidating its employees . . . threatening, assaulting, beating, or preventing any labor organization from distributing literature . . . interfering or coercing employees in their right to organize, or bargain collectively. . . ." The Board further ordered the reinstatement of men who allegedly had been fired for union activity.

The whole affair was not without parallel in those days of labor's resurgence when die-hard employers made their last stands. The singular feature of Ford's

resistance was that it endured so long. This was testimony to Ford's great power, his country-wide reputation for fair treatment of his workers, and the effective-
ness of Bennett's army. It is also highly possible,
though the labor writers do not concede this, that
many Rouge workers were reluctant to throw in their
lot with an organization of which, apparently, in 1937
they knew little. In any case, it was four years after
the overpass fracas that the final showdown came and
labor staged one of the most spectacular strikes in
American labor history.

During this time Ford and Bennett continued their
recalcitrance. Ford had successfully defied N.R.A.,
and he believed he could also prevent N.L.R.B. from
forcing his capitulation. He had come to think of himself as above the law. He was also still confident of
popular support. And, indeed, as late as 1940 a
Fortune poll among working people throughout the
nation showed 75.6 per cent believing that he had
been "helpful to labor"—a higher percentage than
that given to Senator Wagner or John L. Lewis.
Finally, early in 1941 the Rouge began work on
defense, and Ford and Bennett here saw a patriotic
argument against labor's interruptions. By then, however, the pressure had grown formidable outside and
the worm within had turned.

In its issue of March 17, 1941, *Time* published a
characteristic story beginning:

Henry Ford, the most famed tycoon alive, was up a
tree this week. The old 'coon had been treed before, but

this time not only Organized Labor, but the U.S. Government was after him. . . .

Most of the limbs on Henry Ford's tree have been lopped off—one of the last ones by the Supreme Court. An NLRB ruling that Mr. Ford had violated the Wagner Act was upheld by the Circuit Court. The Supreme Court declined to review the case when Ford appealed.

From this last ditch Harry Bennett issued what may have been the most extraordinary statement of his career.

If the NLRB orders an election [he said], of course we will hold one, because Mr. Ford will observe the law. C.I.O. will win it, of course, because it always wins these farcical elections, and we will bargain until Hell freezes over, but they won't get anything.

This announcement—recalling Henry's onetime remark that the purchaser of a Model T might have his car painted any color so long as it was black— could scarcely have deterred the U.A.W. from an act that they must now have believed would be backed by majority public opinion.

The Rouge was struck at midnight on April 1, 1941. The match that set off the carefully laid fuse was the discharge of eight workers for union agitation. It was not an inside "sit-down." The strikers assembled outside the plant.

By early morning [wrote William Simonds in his biography of Henry Ford] picket lines had been established and barricades erected. . . . About the only way one could get into the plant was by parachute from an overhead plane. Trucks and cars guarded the bridge over the Rouge River so that Ford boats could not come up to it to the great docks.

Policeman Harry Bennett telegraphed to President Roosevelt:

Unlawful sit-down strikes, followed by seizure of highway approaches and entrances to the plant in a Communistic demonstration of violence and terrorism have prevented the vast majority of our 85,000 employees from going to work at the Rouge Plant. . . . Communist leaders are actively directing this lawlessness.

The president did not respond. He may have had other information about U.A.W. leadership. The intervention of Governor Van Wagoner of Michigan brought about negotiations between the company and C.I.O.'s Philip Murray. The strike ended, an election was held, and seventy per cent of the Ford workers voted for C.I.O.

Completely defeated, Henry Ford made a characteristic gesture. He offered terms far more generous to labor than those the union had demanded. He wrote both the closed shop and the check-off into the contract—concessions other companies had not made.

Decision by Mr. Ford [wrote Simonds] to enter into the contract with the CIO was based on his faith in the men working for him.

Other writers hold other views. As for "entering into the contract," it hardly seems as if Ford had a wide choice. The generosity of his terms was something else again. Even here the perennial enemies detected ulterior motives. In any case, the agreement was a prodigious "example" to his competitors and, no doubt, caused them some dismay. Over this the old man probably chuckled.

With the arrival of his seventy-eighth birthday the shadow of the war cloud was heavy over the Rouge, and as winter came it was evident that the most gigantic job Ford's or any other company had ever undertaken was close at hand.

IX

MORE than any other single man, it was Henry Ford who made it possible for the United States to become the "arsenal of democracy" in the Second World War. This was not because of the contribution of Ford Motor Company plants to military production in that war. Theirs was only one of many. It was because through the manufacture of twenty million cars over some forty years Ford had evolved a certain pattern for all large-scale production including that of the atomic bomb.

The beautiful detail of this system was designed by engineers of the stature of Charles Sorensen, Peter Edward Martin, and William Knudsen and developed by a host of technicians and craftsmen. But the creative impulse, the direction, and the command, the selection of method and the elimination of non-essentials, and, finally, the relentless drive, were one man's contribution. This might be called the art rather than the science of mass production. It was Henry Ford's gift to the world. In the five years following 1940 it brought success to the arms he hated but the military victory went, after all, to a coalition most of whose members believed in their various ways that they were fighting for freedom.

The elements of the Ford revolution were a century and a half old. The idea of making the parts of

machines interchangeable so that the machines could
be assembled at random was first put into practice by
Eli Whitney in 1798. From the crude muskets he
made on that plan through the classic sequence of the
Colt revolver, the McCormick harvester, the Singer
sewing machine, and the Pope bicycle, the plan had
become more and more co-ordinated. But Henry Ford
gave it a new form.

The essence of that form was motion and continuity. The moving assembly line changed the whole of
the former structure. It set the pace for all the moving
sub-assembly lines that came, at an angle, into it. Once
that long conveyor started moving, everything in the
factory had to move and move continuously. Every
part of the motor car had to be made at once so as to
be ready at the right moment to take its place on the
chassis.

So far, however, the Ford plan could not have created either the magnitude or the pace of American
production in World War II. It could turn out cars
with unprecedented speed. But until the entire nation
became the factory, the scale would be inadequate.
By 1940 this had become a possibility. By then the
Ford Motor Company had long since burst the seams
of any plant. Once upon a time assembly and sub-
assemblies had been contained in Highland Park.
Now even the great Rouge contained only a fraction
of the operation. The sub-assemblies, with their lines
of machines feeding into the chassis line, were no
longer compact in a set of buildings. They were in

cities wide apart, scattered from coast to coast. Parts could be made anywhere, assembled somewhere else. The long-established Ford practice of making parts in Dearborn for a car to be assembled, say, in Copenhagen was subject to infinite expansion.

By 1940 the Ford revolution had spread through all the automotive industry. General Motors, Chrysler, Packard, Willys—every manufacturer had taken over the Ford techniques entire and added new ones in accord with the great pattern. It had affected many other kinds of manufacture. Its decentralizing possibilities had been eagerly seized upon in England, where the "bits and pieces" plan was well adapted to the short hauls in transportation and the multitude of small machine shops.

The final achievement of the Ford revolution, however, was the total isolation of the worker's mind. This has been bitterly and perhaps rightly attacked by sociologists, but it made possible the secrecy with which the atomic bomb and certain other weapons were produced. An assembly-line worker had by 1940 become wholly divorced from his end product. There was no longer any connection between his tightening of a single bolt and the motor car driving off the line thirty operations away. If, instead of an automobile, a tank, a tractor, or a three-inch gun had come off the line it would have made no difference to the man whose sole job was to tighten a bolt. With the same workmen any of these machines could have come off the line and, in the wartime, did.

This meant that a worker could do his job without knowing what he was making or why the man next him did what he did. Thus it became possible to employ thousands of people in the production of a secret weapon without the purpose of their work ever becoming known to any of them. This could not have been done in the First World War. It was possible in the Second only because the Ford revolution, with all its far-reaching consequences, had intervened.

Actually, Henry Ford himself, seventy-six when the war broke in Europe, did not make full use of the potentials of his own creation until long after Pearl Harbor. It seems as if the old man did not realize the power of the complex he had assembled. At his own Rouge, as we shall see, war work was jerky and slow, often interrupted, and occasionally reversed—partly because of the prejudices, stubbornnesses, and whims he injected. Meanwhile, other great industrial entities leaped ahead with the very methods Ford had taught them and brought about a national rhythm into which eventually, under Sorensen's leadership, the Ford company also introduced its stupendous beat.

As he had hated World War I, Henry Ford loathed World War II. In 1939 he was hoping for a stalemate or that the two warring coalitions would destroy each other. Until America entered the war he allied himself with the isolationists: with Charles Lindbergh, even with Robert McCormick, owner of the

old enemy *Tribune*. He was harshly criticized for
having received in 1938 a decoration from Hitler—
thought to be a reward for his onetime anti-Semitism
—and for employing the German–American Bund
leader Fritz Kuhn in a Ford plant.

In the desperate spring of 1940 William Knudsen,
then advisor to the Council for National Defense in
Washington, offered Ford a contract for nine thousand Rolls-Royce engines for British planes. Henry
refused, though the deal was said to be favored by both
Sorensen and Edsel. He refused because Britain was
a belligerent in the war. He would make anything the
United States government might need as a defense
item. But he would make nothing for one of the warring powers, though Knudsen, on getting word of his
refusal, flew to Dearborn to try to persuade him.

In the summer, however, he let Sorensen go to
Hartford to study the Pratt and Whitney Wasp engines for American planes and endorsed Sorensen's
blueprint for a thirty-seven-million-dollar plant at
Dearborn to turn them out. This was the beginning
of the Ford company's real participation in war work.
In carrying it out, Sorensen soared to the greatest height
of his career so far and reached a point from which the
take-off into bomber production was feasible. Yet even
then, when the imminence of American entrance into
the war was setting the whole industrial machine of
the nation into new motion, Henry's idealism kept
war and defense rigidly apart. For American defense,

he boasted in that same summer, he would build a thousand planes a day, and he actually stated that he could do it!

Sorensen, so experienced in mass-production techniques that he could extend them into wholly new fields, began in October 1940 to think not only about engines but about the airplanes themselves. Though Henry Ford did not yet know it, there was little connection between building a 1941-model Ford and a B-24 bomber on an assembly line. Sorensen was fully aware that the things differed not only in size but in kind. A bomber had thirty thousand components. A component in automobile manufacture is, for example, a cylinder block or any embryo, so to speak, of a subassembly—a thing that is put on a conveyor to be machined and finished by a machine sequence and to have parts added to it. Counting nuts, bolts, and screws, it was estimated that 488,193 separate parts went into a B-24 or Liberator bomber. But these parts had to be added to wings or fuselage or tail in a wholly different way from that in which a car was assembled. One reason for this was in the amount and nature of the delicate electrical communication and control equipment. Another was that, while the main assembly of a car consists in hanging things on the chassis as it moves in a straight line, there was no such basic unit on a bomber that could be conveyed from team to team.

It may be compared [writes Christy Borth in his *Masters of Mass Production*] to an industrial attempt to

manufacture houses on an assembly line. The prefabri-
cated rooms would have to be so exactly proportioned
that, when brought together in the assembly plant, they
could be coupled to one another with positive fits at all
cleavage lines of floors, ceilings and walls, and at all con-
tact points of their wiring, piping and so forth.

Sorensen discovered this in January when Knudsen
had him and Edsel flown with some Ford engineers
to San Diego to see how Consolidated Aircraft did it.
They did it, he saw at once, all wrong. On their plan
they could, theoretically, turn out fifty bombers a
month. As President Roosevelt, in May 1940, had
issued a call for fifty thousand airplanes it did not seem
to him that Consolidated's part of the production was
adequate, even if, as was planned, Ford should build
the sub-assemblies and ship them to San Diego to be
put together.

After his first visit Sorensen went to his San Diego
hotel room and tried to think the thing out. He was at
it all night. As a *Fortune* article tells:

The day had been discouraging. Together with Edsel
Ford and . . . Rube Fleet then President of Consolidated Aircraft, he had paced that company's factory
where the B-24 four-engine bomber was struggling toward quantity production. He had seen men falling over
each other working in the suffocating confines of nose and
tail assemblies. He had seen fuselage and center-wing
sections being mated together under the open California
sky, subject to distorting changes of temperature. And
he had come to the conclusion that despite the effort and

enthusiasm and skill being thrown into the work, these methods would not do. If Ford was to come in on the job as Knudsen suggested, it would have to come in on a bigger, planned, semi-mass-production scale.

In the course of the night Sorensen came to the conclusion that the schedule of a bomber a day would never meet the president's demand. Why not, he thought, a bomber an hour?

That was the way Henry had thought back in the days when Sorensen had first come to him. He would multiply other men's top estimates on car production by five or ten. Now, following in the tradition, "Cast-iron Charlie" was thinking the same way about this colossal monster of the air. Why not? Let him make the plans and it could be done. Sorensen and his assistant made sketches. By breakfast they had drawn not only production layouts but the first plans for a factory a mile long and a quarter of a mile wide. But Knudsen had talked only of Ford making parts— maybe, he hinted, they would assemble a few planes. Nonsense, Sorensen thought. By the time this war got under way, Ford would be making whole bombers, one an hour. So the mile-long factory would not be in California; it would be in Michigan, as near as convenient to the Rouge.

He took his sketches home. Before the ground had fully thawed, work on the building began. It was at Willow Run, outside of Ypsilanti, twenty miles west of Dearborn on some of Henry's holdings. It was a quiet sleepy place not precisely adapted to the inva-

sion of some thirty thousand men and women workers.
The eager critics had fun with the name. Willit
Run? they asked. And there were reasons for the
punning question.

The ground was broken in April 1941; the mile-
long, sixty-five-million-dollar plant started production
in May 1942. Yet on August 17 *Life* announced:

> Ford's Willow Run plant . . . advertised the world
> over as a symbol of U.S. industrial might, has not com-
> pleted one plane on its assembly lines and is working
> now at a fraction of capacity.

In the same issue, the story was told of unwilling-
ness on the part of Henry Ford and Harry Bennett
to face the housing problem involved in the enormous
influx of labor into the little college town of Ypsilanti.
They were so opposed to a Federal project for a
"Bomber City" that they sent men out into the fields
to pull up the stakes surveyors had set out.

> This ended [explained the article] the most ambitious
> effort towards solving Detroit's incredible housing
> mess. . . . It is now impossible to rent a decent house
> within 50 miles of the city. Around Willow Run hun-
> dreds of tents, trailers and shacks have sprung up in the
> woods, fields, barnyards.

Henry was quoted as saying his objections to the
Federal project were that "it was a waste of money
and materials" and that "it would concentrate people
where they might be bombed." *Life* added, however,

that Henry's enemies thought he was afraid it would concentrate too many Democrats in Republican Washtenaw County, and Bennett's implacable hostility to the New Deal gives plausibility to the claim. In any case, Ford's performance undoubtedly complicated labor difficulties in the new plant and contributed to a morale that was reported to be the "worst in Detroit." At about the same time, on his seventyninth birthday, he was quoted as being optimistic about the war, which he thought would soon be over.

Sorensen did not think so. But Sorensen had counted without his host—which was the War Department—when he set up the bomber plant. He knew that the mass production of bombers was a very different business from the mass production of cars, trucks, or tanks. He had not realized that bomber designs were impossible to "freeze." They were even harder to freeze than automobile designs had been at the beginning of the Ford story. War planes were still, in this third year of the Second World War, in an experimental phase. This was especially true of American planes less than a year after the United States had gone in. Sorensen found that pilots taking the planes into combat would continually find new "bugs" in them. After the tooling had all been done at Willow Run and the expensive dies cast, the War Department would order radical changes. New special-purpose machines would then have to be built. Sorensen's magnificent jigs and fixtures—the biggest ever built, some of them over sixty feet long—would have to be scrapped.

These things were no one's fault. The war was simply showing up fallacies in the beautiful mass-production pattern. It is hardly surprising that motor manufacturers and automotive engineers, geared to rigid standardization—at least for one model—did not foresee the upsets war would cause. Sorensen's difficulties were increased by the fact that, being a devotee of cast steel, he had made steel dies instead of the soft dies adopted by other motor-makers. This was in the Ford tradition. Nothing was better for producing a million or so identical parts. But they were inflexible when the changes came, and had to be thrown away.

The things that were no one's fault combined with the things that were someone's fault to engender a condition by July 1943 that brought harsh criticism from the Committee Investigating the National Defense Program. Bomber production was far below promises and expectations. Even parts manufacture had been inadequate. Worker morale was still low and absenteeism high. Worst of all, the Truman Committee congratulated General Motors, Ford's top rival, on its part in the war effort!

The year 1943 was, however, a momentous one. In it several things happened, some of them tragic. But in it, too, the crisis was met and passed; from that point the company forged ahead. And at that point, also, the decline of its great dictator began.

War takes almost as heavy a toll from the middle-aged men who labor on the home front as it does from the boys in combat. The number of true war casualties among men too old to fight has never been properly estimated. In the government offices, hours were forgotten, lights burned all night, men and women staggered to rest often less than half alive. In industry the strain was increased by incessant conflict with government, by enemy scrapping of the most careful plans, by breakdowns in the delivery of materials, by endless waste.

Peter Martin had survived all the Ford purges from the beginning of the company. He could not survive the war. His heart had failed in 1941. By 1943 his brilliant work was finished; he was awaiting death, which came the following year.

Edsel succumbed in May 1943 to intestinal trouble for which he had had an operation some sixteen months before. From the first planning of the bomber program, he had given it far more of his time, effort, and worry than the state of his health could stand. He was halfway through his fiftieth year.

His life had always been more or less frustrated. His father had won most of the disagreements between them. From his father's tastes he had usually diverged. He had recoiled from much of the ruthlessness he had seen in the great empire. He had maintained a view of labor wholly opposite from that which Bennett shared with his father. The rank and file of the workers thought of him as their champion.

Henry Ford's shadow so obscured Edsel that no adequate estimate of him by writers or public has emerged. He has been sketched as a "nice fellow" with gentle manners, unfortunate as the son of a giant whose stature he could not have approached even had he been permitted to grow up to the full measure of his ideals. Actually, he attained a kind of greatness that Henry was utterly incapable of understanding. He lacked his father's mechanical talent and interest, nor had he the sort of shrewdness that accompanied some of Henry's celebrated coups. He had, however, a statesmanlike quality that reached far beyond the industrial confines of his day. His thinking was a long way ahead of his time. We are moving today toward the sort of world he envisioned, a world in which men are waking to the responsibilities of industry to society and in which the whole field of human relations is changing. Edsel saw this world clearly: he saw an interdependence of production and the social, political, and economic factors in world civilization in which the parochial concepts of Henry Ford can find no place. In these days when so many industrialists are playing a part in government and international affairs, Edsel would have found his ideal niche. In the already obsolete Ford dictatorship of 1943, where the old man was the unique law, there was no direction for his talents.

Edsel had been at odds with Harry Bennett from the beginning of Bennett's power. At his death he had many partisans throughout the hierarchy among men who were aware of the hot struggle for power at the top. His son was, after all, the heir apparent and would one day be caught in the struggle that had been so hard for Edsel.

For a long time he had been president of the company in name. But he never had the full power of his office. His decisions were altered or sometimes reversed—not always by his father, but with his father's silent consent.

We are not told much about the father's grief at his son's death. Perhaps he was numbed by it or by his eighty years. We are told that, after Edsel died, Bennett conducted a purge of those in the company who had taken Edsel's part and that the old man did nothing to stop it. If this is true, it was unwise of Bennett, with Edsel's son standing as he did so close to the threshold. Possibly the old man let Bennett have his fling, knowing that in the end a Ford would enter and take control.

Edsel's death occurred at what many thought was the all-time low of the Ford Motor Company. The report of the Truman Committee came soon after in midsummer. In the fall the tide turned. Rumor said the improvement came because Ford was scared. Rumor said that, unless Ford production improved, the government would take over and run the plant.

It seems highly improbable that this was why things changed. It is far more reasonable to believe that, after trial and error, Sorensen and the brilliant men he commanded had learned to master the quick changes; that production lines had become more flexible. One of Henry's last acts before Edsel died was to spread the industry over the country—following the logical growth of the mass-production plan—subcontracting everywhere for parts. Into the net were drawn the smallest shops. If the machines at Willow Run were not adapted to some new operation, it was probable that somewhere in the country there were tools that could do the job. As 1944 came in, this decentralization was beginning to take place throughout industry, and by the end of the war it looked as if every lathe or planer, every drill and milling machine, was shaping some part that would travel along to a main assembly to finish a bomber or fighter, a tank, a gun, or a ship.

As production bettered, worker morale went up. Then new methods of handling labor were learned and put into practice. By January 1944 Sorensen's production schedule of one Liberator an hour was passed.

Then, suddenly, Sorensen was there no more. In March he was out of the company he had served so brilliantly for forty years. Few of the people who knew the score in the company believed that he resigned because of ill-health. It was easier to believe that, big as the Ford empire had grown, it was not big enough to hold both Charlie Sorensen and Harry Bennett.

And Bennett had become far too important to Henry Ford for Henry to let him go, though he had been there only twenty-seven years to Sorensen's forty.

The *Detroit Free Press* came out with the flat statement that Henry himself had fired Sorensen.

This was as shocking to some motormen [*Time* commented the following week] as if the wizard of Dearborn had slashed off his own right arm.

Sorensen had been on vacation "fishing in the Bahamas" when the blow came. It was true that, having geared Willow Run to one of the great production miracles of the war, he had been tired. But when he called reporters to his Miami house to tell them the news they noted that he was "tanned and looking fit."

"I am compelled [he said] to take a much needed rest."

Time concluded its story by saying that:

there is no one in the empire now—outside of Henry and Henry II, Ford vice-president—to challenge the absolute power of . . . Harry Bennett.

The "weekly news magazine" was prescient in its exceptions. It did not know much about the vice-president. No one did. Henry Ford II had just come onto the Board. When his father died he had been called out of the Navy to sit there. He was twenty-seven years old. Harry Bennett, whose men had guarded him in his pram, was hardly afraid of him.

After three months "Cast-Iron Charlie" was sufficiently recovered to accept the presidency of WillysOverland Motors and continue there with backbreaking war work.

By the end of the war some eight thousand heavy bombers had rolled off the Willow Run line and taken the air. Coupled with a tremendous output of jeeps, tanks, and other military transport machines at the Rouge, this record showed that, as it always had, the Ford company had come through in the end, making so brilliant a recovery that, from the V-J Day view, it hardly seemed that it could have made too many and too serious mistakes.

In the summer of 1945, however, the master was rarely seen. Visitors who so short a time before had watched the lithe octogenarian vaulting over fences or staging for the astonished caller a fifty-yard dash did not find him at the Rouge or in any of his accustomed haunts in Dearborn. Officially he had retired. Perhaps he was spending most of his time sitting on the spacious terrace of Fair Lane, watching the curving river and dreaming of past glories. When a photograph of him appeared, taken in 1946 as he sat in the precious relic of his first car with Clara beside him and his big grandson standing behind the little buggy, those who had known him studied his face and thought for the first time: "How old he is!" It was rumored that his mind was no longer always clear.

In the fall they stopped looking for him. The boy

was in his office. The official announcement simply said that the Board of Directors had elected him president. But the belief persisted that even in this dim twilight of his life the Board would not act without the old man's nod, and that Henry had gone further and said that the new president should, unlike his father, have complete control and final command. Perhaps Clara and Edsel's widow had prevailed on him not to delay.

The world watched the boy. Would Bennett be a sort of regent? Would a coalition of the old guard come and take the lad in hand, show him the ropes, flatter him, wheedle him, advise him, and then retire into the shadow behind the throne and see that he worked their will? The stage was set for such an act. No one saw anything particularly brilliant in this grandson. His career to date had been colorless. His scholarship had been indifferent. He had left Yale without graduating, apparently because it bored him. Where was that vanadium-steel will that had made this lad's grandfather the most powerful industrialist in all history?

Perhaps Henry II did not know the answer to this when he assumed power. He did know, however, very definitely that his power would never come to fruition as long as certain factions remained in the Rouge.

It is quite a thing for a man under thirty to fire a thousand employees as soon as he becomes boss. Yet that is what Henry Ford II did. Some were enemies of his father. Many were appointees of Bennett. Some were dead wood. When the war was over, the company was found, for all its technical efficiency, to be weak in its administrative direction. There had been too much whim in the hiring and firing of lieutenants. Purges had got to be a sort of game.

This one was not part of the game. It was the beginning of one of those extraordinary resurgences that had always come in the low moments of this company's history—and just in time.

It was said that a thousand employees left after Henry II came in. And one of the first to go—only a few weeks after the young man's election—was Harry Herbert Bennett.

Not a whisper came from Fair Lane. For a year there were none of the old pronouncements. It was forgotten that cigarette-smoking led to prison, that milk was poisonous, that people were reincarnated, that salt was good for the hair, that reading can become a dope habit, that charity resulted from misguided impulses. . . .

Then on the seventh of April, 1947, news came again from Fair Lane, and every wheel stopped turning for a day in the Rouge, and in every factory in the state of Michigan the workers stood silent for one minute. In Greenfield Village a hundred thousand persons came to look at the relaxed face of the man who had remade the physical world.

X

THE ATTEMPTS to understand and explain Henry
Ford have been legion; none is adequate. When all
is told, questions stand unanswered, knots remain tied,
and loose ends hang unconnected. The descriptions,
the stories, the reported conversations by those who
knew him best contradict one another. One will tell
of kindness to an ailing or crippled child, another of
cruelty to a faithful employee; one of sentiment, another of disloyalty. There were authenticated cases of
individual gifts fantastically generous against a background of rigid opposition to charity. There are anecdotes of prodigious memory and of overnight forgetting; of shyness and of aggression; of long patience
and of destructive haste; of stubborn persistence and
of a multitude of unfinished and abandoned business.

Perhaps in time, when the abundant material is
all explored, the parts can be assembled and made to
fit into some sort of synthesis. Meanwhile, we shall
have to look at the various interpretations guessed at
by those who have watched him and worked with
him, heard his voice, and caught the alternating flashes
of greatness and littleness as his thought jumped.

In Henry Ford's face Allan Benson, a Detroit
journalist, saw two personalities:

One is diffident, almost to the point of bashfulness,
yet very friendly. . . . He had a way of entering that

seemed almost noiseless and instantaneous—I looked up and there he was. He was always smiling as he approached and his eyes were looking to the side and toward the floor. . . . I was always reminded of the good-natured schoolboy called to the front of the classroom to shake hands with a visitor and just a trifle embarrassed about it. . . .

It is the boyish, smiling, youthful Ford that enters the office. In ten seconds, and for no apparent reason, the smile may flit from his face and you behold a man who, from his eyes up, seems as old as the pyramids. Many little wrinkles dart out sidewise from his eyes. The skin is stretched rather tightly over his brow, and on each temple is a little vein resembling a corkscrew.

Ford made much the same impression on Dean Marquis, who perhaps knew him better than anyone outside his family.

The baffling thing in him [Marquis wrote in *Henry Ford: An Interpretation*] is the puzzling mixture of opposing natures.

There rages in him an endless conflict between ideals, emotions and impulses as unlike as day and night,—a conflict that makes one feel that two personalities are striving within him for mastery. . . .

These variations in mental moods are generally accompanied by outward changes. . . . Today he stands erect, lithe, agile, full of life, happy as a child, and filled with the child spirit of play. Out of his eyes there looks . . . a soul that is affable, gentle, kindly, generous to a fault. But tomorrow he may be the opposite. He will have the appearance of a man shrunken by long illness.

The shoulders droop. . . . His face is deeply lined, and the lines are not such as go to make up a kindly, open countenance. The affable, gentle manner has disappeared. There is a light in the eye that reveals a fire burning within altogether unlike that which burned there yesterday. He has the appearance of a man utterly wearied and exhausted yet driven on by a relentless and tireless spirit.

The title of Benson's book, *The New Henry Ford*, suggests that some sort of fundamental change took place in him at some point in his career. The book, however, was published in 1923 and at that time Ford's widened social and political interests suggested a kind of rebirth or altered character. But as we review his life as a whole it is obvious that there never was a "new Henry Ford." In an afternoon he might seem new to one who had met him in the morning. After Monday's Henry, Tuesday's was new, perhaps. But the basic prejudices remained. Men came into and went out of his affections and confidence, but his convictions about categories of people stuck: the common man was good; aristocrats, bankers, and professional politicians were bad.

Circumstances forced on him certain superficial changes that were regarded by critical biographers as indicating deterioration or departure from early principles. It is pointed out that from a simple home life he moved into a kind of palace set in the midst of spacious grounds, manned by a large corps of domestic employees. But this elaboration—which has been grossly exaggerated—resulted from the kind of persecution from which the very rich always suffer, especially when a saintly halo has been added by popular fancy to the wealth.

Probably Henry Ford [writes C. B. Glasscock in *The Gasoline Age* in 1937] would still be living in the unpretentious house in Detroit which he occupied during the early days of his success, if that very success had not brought around him a crowd of sycophants, beggars and nuisances which necessitated his removal for self-protection. That home was ample for his comfort and for the informal entertainment of the few old friends in whose society he was at ease. He had no desire for extravagant luxury or display. But when his success attained a point which brought his name to the attention of the world, he awoke to find a crowd before his house every day. It was a crowd of self-seekers attempting to reach him with scores of appeals for charity, for jobs, for financial support or approval of gadgets of invention. He was literally driven from his old home to a new and elaborate estate at Dearborn where extensive gardens, walls and guards could assure him protection and privacy.

In a sense Fair Lane was a kind of prison. At the entrance to the long drive through woods and fields to the house a continuous guard screened all who sought entrance. Only the intimates of the family were admitted. But those who, since Ford's death, have seen Fair Lane (which now contains the celebrated Ford Archives) can find little of the ornate embellishment so familiar in the residences of great wealth. The house is severe, unbeautiful; its furniture lacks not only the attributes of luxury but often those of comfort; although, probably because convention demanded it, the architect included a bowling alley and swimming pool, these remained unused. The domestic staff was small, its people old and faithful, lacking in either "smartness" or servility. Henry would never have a valet. "I still like boiled potatoes with the skins on," Marquis quotes him as saying, "and I don't want a man standing back of my chair at table laughing up his sleeve at me while I am taking the potatoes' jackets off."

It was thought that his attitude toward labor changed; that he drove his workers harder as the company grew more successful and that, in the plant, brutality replaced humane treatment. Marquis, who entered Ford's employ in 1915 and left it in 1921, saw the discharge during that period of those executives "who at times set justice and humanity above profits and production" and saw them replaced by men to whom "the sole end of industry was production and profits, and the one sure way of getting these things out of labor was to curse it, threaten it, drive it, insult it, humiliate it and discharge it on the slightest provocation."

Although some new production men undoubtedly brought attitudes that resulted in brutal incidents, there does not seem to have been much change in Ford's own belief from the beginning that labor should be handled without gloves. Perhaps the worst accusations ever made accompanied the accolades about the five-dollar day in 1914, when it was said that the "speeded-up" assembly turned out almost as many nervous wrecks as cars. From the beginning Ford was a hard master. Even in his doctored autobiography *My Life and Work* the attempt to modify his own pronouncements to this effect are never quite convincing.

A great business [he stated] is really too big to be human. It grows so large as to supplant the personality of the man. In a big business the employer, like the employee, is lost in the mass.

He said the Ford Company did not believe in the "glad hand" or the professional "personal touch" or "human element," and added the statement—surprising to the reader in the mid-1950's—that "it is too late in the day for that sort of thing."

I pity the poor fellow who is so soft and flabby that he must always have "an atmosphere of good feeling" around him before he can do his work. There are such men. And in the end, unless they obtain enough mental and moral hardiness to lift them out of their soft reliance on "feeling," they are failures.

This statement, and not the pussyfooting paragraph that follows it and pulls its punch with a definition (probably Crowther's) of "feeling," comes straight from the shoulder of the true Henry Ford. But how many industrialists of his day whose behavior has stuffed the grievance record of organizing labor have been willing to disclose so harsh a code and let it stand in print?

There was nothing new in these views of Ford's. "The idea," wrote E. G. Pipp in *Henry Ford—Both Sides of Him*, "that Ford was adored by his men has certainly never existed except outside Detroit." Yet in the plant, too, there were individual cases of justice and even mercy toward his workers. Often they were dictated by respect for the worker's achievements, as in the case of the talented homosexual whom he furnished with a private laboratory where he would not be persecuted by his fellow workers. And even Ford's hard critics concede his occasional personal interest in cases of illness, injury, or misfortune among his workers. That these may have been motivated by the moment's whim is probable, yet even this modifies the monstrous picture.

He took a firm stand against organized charity—a position often taken in later years by many would-be reformers.

I have no patience with professional charity or with any kind of commercialized humanitarianism. The moment human helpfulness is systematized, organized, commercialized, and professionalized, the heart of it is extinguished, and it becomes a cold and clammy thing.

He added the trenchant observation that "the recipient of bounty feels that he has been belittled in the taking, and it is a question whether the giver should not also feel that he has been belittled in the giving." Counterbalancing his disapproval of formulated giving, Ford expresses his belief that the underprivileged and the disabled can be put to work as never before.

The subdivision of industry opens places that can be filled by practically any one. There are more places in subdivision industry that can be filled by blind men than there are blind men. There are more places that can be filled by cripples than there are cripples. And in each of these places the man who shortsightedly might be considered as an object of charity can earn just as adequate a living as the keenest and most able-bodied. It is a waste to put an able-bodied man in a job that might be just as well cared for by a cripple. It is a frightful waste to put the blind at weaving baskets.

It was largely Henry Ford who—unconsciously, perhaps, until it was called to his attention—made possible these opportunities throughout industry. Any visitor to the Rouge plant must remember seeing disabled men and women at work there. Those who find it difficult to speak any good of Henry Ford are quick to point out that this is a publicity trick arranged to cover dark abuses. If it is such, it is publicity that is valuable to society, whatever the motive. The demonstration that this thing is possible—even if there were but a single exhibit—by Ford and other employers of labor has wrought great changes in the dark world of the defective. Today the principle is everywhere in practice and the helpless blind man, deaf-mute, or amputee enjoys self-respect and earning capacity.

One of the objects sometimes pointed to as a refutation of Ford's theory about charity is the Henry Ford Hospital in Detroit. He took this over abruptly when the subscriptions for a general city hospital were running low. About it many apocryphal stories grew up. One was that he had gone into a rage over a doctor's bill and resolved to furnish reasonable medical care. One said that he had some plan of putting patients, like cars, on an assembly line. Still another persistent rumor told that it was built and operated to give free treatment to Ford employees. His own account stated:

This hospital is designed to be self-supporting—to give a maximum of service at a minimum of cost and without the slightest colouring of charity. . . .

In the new buildings we have erected there are no wards. All of the rooms are private and each one is provided with a bath. The rooms . . . are all identical in size, in fittings, and in furnishings. There is no choice of rooms . . . of anything within the hospital.

The hospital may not have had the color of charity, but it certainly had the color of socialized medicine and it produced an uproar among Detroit physicians. The hospital doctors and nurses were on salary and had no outside patients. The patients' fees included medical attention; operations were extra, but at fixed charges. There were no free beds or clinics.

After a period of vicissitudes, during which it was both justly and unjustly attacked, the Henry Ford Hospital, according even to the skeptic, Keith Sward, became one of the foremost medical institutions in the Middle West.

The tales of Ford's individual kindnesses and whimsical personal charities would fill as large a volume as those demonstrating his hardness of heart. One that has something of special charm and seems typical of the gentler incidents that must often have furnished interludes in the long spans of toughness is told by William C. Richards in *The Last Billionaire*.

The 14-year old daughter of an executive became unaccountably ill and lost fifty pounds. Weeks passed before the cause—a fall that resulted in a glandular upset—was discovered.

Unpasteurized milk was prescribed. He iced and delivered it each morning from his own herd. Tomato juice was recommended. Cases arrived from Ford. He was on the phone solicitously. One Friday morning he appeared at her home on his bicycle. Was she strong enough to attend an old fashioned dancing party he was giving the same evening? . . .

The patient brightened perceptibly at the idea. . . . A service man rang the doorbell an hour later. In his hand was a single yellow rose—"for the little miss to wear tonight." The squire of Fair Lane had gone straight to his gardens to give a discouraged young lady a little extra buoyancy.

According to Richards, he was "a push-over for any newspaper sob story." Seeing a photograph of an eviction, he was likely to send the family an embarrassingly generous gift. He got a house for one family of eight the day of their eviction and sent his own men to paint and decorate it. He was always remembering someone who had done him a kindness in his difficult days and rewarding him or his heirs with a new Model T. A story tells of his sending a new car to some college boys whose jalopy was in a ditch as he drove by. He is said to have called out "Get a horse" to them, but a few weeks later a local Ford dealer delivered to one of them a new Ford. Henry had taken the car's license number, found the owner's name, and sent in the order.

The stories are easy to tell. Often enough we come on a chestnut that has been told about a dozen others —such as the one about his saying to the Queen of Rumania: "Queen, meet our Mr. Black." The likelihood is, however, that enough of them are true— some, indeed, can be documented—to show a trend. There can be little doubt that Ford shared this sporadic, unreasoned largesse with other rich men; it is also likely that it never became a habit and that a good deal of the private charity was calculated to be productive. In the shop most of it proved so.

This brings us back to the reported cruelties in the plants, where it was felt, as Marquis said, that the one sure way to get production and profits was to curse, threaten, drive, insult, and so on. If such brutalities actually prevailed, we are compelled to the dismal conclusion that this *was* a "sure way" to get production, because never in recorded history was such production got as in the plants that were making Model T. The facts leave the student wondering. We know that some of the devices of Bennett's later regime were rightly condemned, but in those days production was low. Is it not reasonable to suspect—with what we know of the success of wise human relations in today's industry—that there were compensations, ameliorations, and attractions in working for Ford? Naturally his men did not "adore" him. Workers have never, since the days of small-unit New England industry, "adored" an employer. Yet whenever he issued a call for workers they answered by the tens of thousands.

One of the primary causes of the failure to get at the true character of Henry Ford is the difficulty of divorcing the facts as they are recorded from the "Ford legend." Other captains of industry had practiced every sort of devious dealings and condoned shocking labor and business relations. The public, hearing of them, had simply nodded: sure enough, such things go on in business; it is too bad, but what can you expect? The targets were really not worth while for the critics to hit; the stories may have been bad enough, but they were not news. Ford, on that day in 1914 when he established a so-called minimum wage of five dollars for eight hours, acquired a halo that transformed him into the perfect target for all the "realists" and debunkers. From that moment until long after he was dead he was always news.

His own avowed belief was that the wage-raise was simply good business. See, said the critics, what Ford does is hypocrisy; it pretends philanthropy, but actually it is simply good business! It was then the custom to do intensive research into Saint Henry's other hypocrisies. He speeded up assembly. He put a six-month qualification clause into the five-dollar minimum—a worker did not get it the day he was hired. So Saint Henry resorted to the devious operation of firing men and rehiring them!

Anyone who had done so radical a thing was fair game for investigation. It was found that he censored the enriched workers' conduct off duty. A five-dollar man must be a moral man, thrifty, sober. This too was good business. Actually, spying on private lives was not peculiar to the Ford company. And the high-handedness of the company police who came later was nothing to that in Aliquippa or Ambridge or Wheeling or Weirton. But Ford must not do these things.

In an ironic article in the *American Mercury* for July 1931 Murray Godwin remembers the denunciation by critical writers of Ford's unloading his cars on the dealers in order to raise the money to repay his bank loan.

Ford raised the money [Godwin says] by arbitrary methods but at least he gave equally saleable goods as security. What if he had lost control [to the bankers]? Within a month or two a mountain of Ford stock would have burdened the country. The present depression would have come sooner and might have been more ruinous.

It was usually recognized that the world of big business was a world apart; that apparently ruthless decisions were often made to avoid large catastrophes. Sometimes there were large injustices, big concerns swallowed little ones, enormous concentrations of power grew up. The liberal journals cried out against these things and a good many people shook their heads about the "tycoons" who did them, but the events were rarely worth more than half a column in the daily press. But Ford was a man apart. He had set himself apart, true enough. A great concert of people, seeing his apartness, canonized him. To the rest he was the incarnate devil—not because of what he did, but against the background of his alleged sainthood. The dichotomy makes the post-mortem analysis—or synthesis—a complex task.

Henry Ford had few close friends. On a marked page of Emerson's essay "Manners" in Ford's annotated copy of the *Essays*, these words occur:

Let us not be too much acquainted. . . . We should meet each morning, as from foreign countries, and spending the day together, should depart at night as into foreign countries. In all things I would have the island of a man inviolate. Let us sit apart as the gods, talking from peak to peak all around Olympus.

Isolation of this sort was an article of faith with Ford and was certainly practiced by him far more than by Emerson. The men closest to him by circumstances in his business he always kept at a distance in personal relationships. Even Harry Bennett entitled his *apologia, We Never Called Him Henry.* His confidential secretary, Liebold, called him Mr. Ford to the end, and Ford was meticulous about "Mr. Liebold." Perhaps his much-publicized cronies, Edison, Burroughs, and Firestone, were exceptions to this rule, though even here first names were probably not used.

There must have been considerable intimacy in this surprisingly varied group. What the magnificently white-bearded naturalist, whose photograph taken in company with Ford and Edison appeared so frequently, found so engaging in the moody and mentally isolated industrialist has never been fully revealed. Ford's attachment to Burroughs, however, is explainable by an old interest in birds and woodland creatures that goes back to Henry's earliest childhood. As for Edison, there seems to have been a one-way current of affection, admiration, and, indeed, at times, worship flowing from Henry. From the time when he first spoke to Edison till the day Edison re-enacted his final experiments with the incandescent lamp in his restored Menlo Park laboratory, which Ford had transported to Dearborn, this adoration never abated. Even after the inventor's death the shrines to Edison in Greenfield Village were evidence of a loyalty he gave no one else with the exception of his wife. Edison furnished an outlet for Ford's most fervent (and sometimes ludicrous) outbursts of sentimentality.

The quadrumvirate, with Harvey Firestone trailing the lions, went on frequent camping trips together. Occasionally they would attach some transient lion such as President Harding. Burroughs entertained Ford in California at the time Ford was pretending he had left his company and was about to launch a rival to Model T. Edison and Ford established adjoining winter homes at Fort Myers, Florida. One of the most noted events of the Ford-Edison friendship was a railway journey over the line on which Edison, as a boy, had peddled newspapers and candy; following along with Ford's penchant for elaborate practical jokes, the middle-aged inventor again marched through the train with a basket. The station on that line at which an irate conductor had thrown the boy Edison off a train for carrying on chemical experiments in a baggage car was later restored and brought to Greenfield Village.

Firestone's connection with the alliance was a more natural one. His acquaintance with Ford began over a tire deal, and Firestone was one of the few businessmen whose relations with the company were maintained on an enduringly friendly basis. Apparently one of the important roles he and Burroughs played on the camping trips was as audience to what Burroughs at least thought were the excruciatingly funny stories told round the fire by Edison and Ford.

There is little question that Edison's influence was dominant in Ford's extra-curricular thinking. His pronouncements on history, education, politics, and re-

ligion were echoes of Edison's own and no less curious. Both men were frequently put in the position of
talking about subjects of which they knew nothing.
Why Edison, for example, should have been asked
what he thought of God and immortality is a journalist's secret. Why both Ford and Edison did not tell
the reporters that these things were none of their
business is easier to understand. Indeed, they went
further. They trumpeted their pronouncements in
chorus without being asked. Edison shouted that
cigarettes had a direct deleterious effect on brain tissue,
and Ford circulated the celebrated tract, *The Little
White Slaver*, among his employees as a kind of
antiphonal response. When Edison expressed his dis-
belief in the next world, Ford said yes, he too would
take "one world at a time." Edison did, it is said,
allow for the possibility of reincarnation and Ford
came to feel sure he had lived before and remembered
certain things.

Whatever the rivals of the Ford company may
have said, there can be no question that Ford's contribution to the world's automobile industry was essential to its success. The main facts are obvious. But a
specific instance in which he not only aided the industry but helped clarify the whole patent complex
was his stubborn fight against the Selden efforts to
dominate all production and sale of motor cars.
Hounded by the A.L.A.M. for years, threatened by
boycott, blackmail, litigation, and every sort of ob-

struction, he said and repeated his resounding No! And it was not as if, in all this time, he spoke from a platform of security or success. At the nadir of the company's history he refused. The reward, when it came in 1911 with the opinion that the Selden patent did not apply to any of the cars then being manufactured, brought a sigh of relief to every motormaker.

And Ford's stand in this matter was not mere stubbornness—the kind of "orneriness" that kept him out of many associations and alliances. It was a certainty that the patent itself was unsound; that any patent that attempted to cover such a combination of inventions should not be allowed. The results of his belief have been a re-examination of many claims and a considerable measure of reform in the Patent Office.

The establishment of Ford assembly plants in Europe brought about much redesign of factories in France, England, Italy, the Scandinavian countries, and, in particular, Russia. While full mass production has never been adopted outside America, there have been many approaches to it in motor-car, tractor, and aircraft manufacture. This can be traced with certainty to Ford.

In Germany, between the wars, "fordism" became at one time almost a religion. At the bottom of Germany's depression the *"Rationalisierung"* that was thought to be the means of salvation was based largely on Ford principles of standardization, continuity, and economy.

The fires of enmity and anger over moral issues must die down before a proper estimate of Henry Ford can be made. Too many personal enemies and admirers are still alive to permit an objective study. We cannot forever discuss the morals or the ethics of a man who contributed such values to our civilization. The time must come when he will be accepted as a great historic fact; not in the light of the rightness or wrongness of his individual acts.

It has been said that he was wholly a product of his time; that what he did would have been possible only in the precise years in which he lived. Government intervention in the affairs of business has ended the possibility of his particular kind of dictatorship. Labor legislation no longer permits the freedoms with workers that are supposed to have enhanced his success. War demands have placed new restrictions on materials; taxes have limited profits.

Many of these observations are true. Ford was not, however, an inevitable product of his time. He was original and revolutionary. He defied precedent. He never once allowed the impossibilities of the past to limit the possibilities of the future.

This, above all, was what he meant when he said that history was bunk.

NOTE ON SOURCES

PROBABLY the most controversial figure in American industrial history, Henry Ford has been the subject of still uncounted books, public documents, pamphlets, magazine and newspaper articles. To compile a bibliography and assemble the various items is one of the tasks which the Archives of the Ford Motor Company at Dearborn has assigned itself, and, though the collection is still incomplete, it is the most comprehensive body of Fordiana now available to students of the life and era of this astonishing American. Much credit is due the archivist and his staff for their objective approach to the problem: the adverse—even violently critical—material is all there along with the honeyed words of the hero-worshippers.

The contradictions in the various biographies are not, however, entirely a matter of opposing views. The more bewildering ones are in the realms of fact. Apparently much of Ford's activity was shrouded in obscurity—or contrived mystery—and some of the factual data are still exceedingly hard to verify. As writing was always difficult for him, he made almost no notes, kept no diary, and used the little memorandum books that, in later life, were constantly with him for misspelled philosophical remarks.

Perhaps of all the mines of misinformation about Henry Ford, his autobiography, *My Life and Work* (Doubleday, Page, 1922), is the deepest. This was apparently dictated in a haphazard way to his amanuensis, Samuel Crowther, who, though he attested on the title

page to his collaboration, seems to have made no attempt to check Ford's prodigious lapses of memory.

Thus in a book that biographers naturally tend to regard as almost a primary source, names, dates, and events
are often merely guessed at. A minimum of checking
would show, for example, that Ford's highly significant
first meeting with Edison occurred not, as the autobiography states, in 1888, three years before he entered the
Edison Company in Detroit, but in 1896. A brief con-
sultation of newspaper files would correct the statement
that it was the "Arrow" in which Ford made his world
record on the ice of Lake St. Clair in January 1904.
Indeed, Ford had in his possession photographs of the
"999" taken during the event—pictures that are now in
the Archives.

More difficult to check is the date of the first Ford
car. The autobiography gives it as 1893, and many
writers—including even the careful Arthur Pound—have
accepted Ford's statement. It is naturally difficult to prove
that Ford had no car in 1893, but there is no documentation to support the claim. Exhaustive research has established the spring of 1896 for the launching of the first Ford.

The best documentation on this and most other early
Ford facts is in *Ford: the Times, the Man, and the
Company* (Scribner's, 1954). This is the first volume
—to 1915—of the most complete work on the subject
thus far attempted.

Of many secondary sources, let us consider the adverse
ones first. Foremost of these is *The Legend of Henry
Ford*—whose very title announces a *parti pris*—by Keith
Sward. Mr. Sward, a former public-relations counsel for
Ford's bitter enemy, the C.I.O., can hardly have been

expected to lean toward objectivity. Nevertheless, though its emphasis is heavily upon Ford's relations with labor, this is by all odds the most complete and documented biography that has yet appeared. The full notes and bibliography are extremely useful to any writer on the subject, and while in his text the author seems often to regard a news story from a Detroit paper as final, he does give his source precisely so that another writer may consult it directly and use his judgment as to its veracity. *The Legend of Henry Ford* was published in 1948 by Rinehart and Company.

Jonathan N. Leonard's *The Tragedy of Henry Ford* (Putnam, 1932), represents Ford as a sort of Franken-stein defeated by his own monsters—a thesis that later developments hardly support. Although the book is without documentation and its accuracy has been questioned, its audience seems to have been large and sympathetic, and it has often been quoted.

Less worthy of serious attention than either of these is Upton Sinclair's *The Flivver King* (Sinclair, 1937), a sensational, highly colored piece of melodrama which has been described as "a socialistic tract, thinly disguised as a biography."

The other attacks are mostly in pamphlet form. E. G. Pipp, one-time editor of the *Dearborn Independent,* published a scathing attack called *The Real Henry Ford* in 1922 (Detroit: *Pipp's Weekly*), but this seems to have been inspired by fears that Ford might be politically successful. Four years later Pipp produced a far more balanced and objective study entitled *Henry Ford: Both Sides of Him* (Detroit: *Pipp's Magazine,* 1926). This has been useful in its appraisal.

"J 8"; a Chronicle of Neglected Truth is a pamphlet by Walter M. Cunningham, a former employee. It is highly partisan, presenting what are supposed to be labor's views, and, as such, it has been taken seriously by Sward and others.

While all these attacks are more or less emotional, they are more interesting and some of them are far more valuable than the eulogies. These include William A. Simonds's *Henry Ford; His Life, His Work, His Genius* (Bobbs-Merrill, 1943); Rose Wilder Lane's *Henry Ford's Own Story* (Ellis O. Jones, 1917); Sarah T. Bushnell's *The Truth about Henry Ford* (Reilly and Lee, 1922); the Ford and Crowther books: *Today and Tomorrow* (Doubleday, Page, 1926) and *Moving Forward* (Doubleday, Doran, 1930); J. G. de R. Hamilton's *Henry Ford; the Man, the Worker, the Citizen* (Holt, 1927); James M. Miller's *The Amazing Story of Henry Ford* (M. A. Donahue, 1922); and William R. Stidger's *Henry Ford; the Man and His Motives* (Doran, 1923).

Only two of these are of any value. Mr. Simonds's book, while heavily slanted, is packed with information, most of it probably correct though undocumented. It has been of considerable help, especially in its details of Ford's early life. Ford and Crowther's *Today and Tomorrow* is more accurate than *My Life and Work* and gives useful and often fascinating information about Ford's extracurricular activities. But even quasi-admirers of Henry Ford must wish that *Moving Forward* had never been published. One may plausibly question whether Ford himself ever read it.

Of the books that both praise and blame, two are

outstanding. These are Samuel S. Marquis's *Henry Ford: an Interpretation* (Little, Brown, 1923) and William C. Richards's *The Last Billionaire* (Scribner's, 1948). Marquis came as near as anyone ever did to being Ford's "spiritual adviser" and knew him more intimately, probably, than anyone outside his immediate family. His book has been valuable as a character study, and several important quotations have been made from it. One might wish, at times, that the Dean had been a better writer. The Richards book is a treasure chest of salty anecdote. It is wholly reportorial and objective, a triumphant achievement. It is not, however, a biography; it is a collection—designedly amorphous and perhaps for that reason casually readable. Some of the stories seem to have been told of others besides Henry, but one senses a wink from the author when they are included.

Impressionistic books that aim at character analysis are Allan L. Benson's *The New Henry Ford* (Funk and Wagnalls, 1923); Charles Merz's *And Then Came Ford* (Doubleday, Doran, 1929); and Garet Garrett's *The Wild Wheel* (Pantheon, 1952).

Much about Ford and the background of his success has been recorded in books on automotive history. The most generally accepted of these is *Men, Money, and Motors* (Harper, 1929), by Theodore F. MacManus and Norman Beasley. It is largely anecdotal. The stories are corroborated by most students of the industry in the 1920's. The book is, however, careless and often confusing in its arrangement, and it bristles with small errors due to cursory proofreading. A more workmanlike job is C. B. Glasscock's *The Gasoline Age* (Bobbs-Merrill, 1937). Ralph Epstein's *The Automobile Industry*

(A. W. Shaw, 1928) is standard: its tables, statistics, and analyses of trends are *sine qua non* for any study of the early days. E. D. Kennedy in *The Automobile Industry* (Reynal and Hitchcock, 1941) carries the history farther. Also dealing with the industry in general but with intentional emphasis on General Motors is Arthur Pound's *The Turning Wheel* (Doubleday, Doran, 1924). Another aspect is carefully explored in Lawrence H. Seltzer's *A Financial History of the American Automobile Industry* (Houghton Mifflin, 1928).

The colorful background material was found in Hiram Maxim's charming *Horseless Carriage Days* (Harper, 1937); Charles B. King's privately printed reminiscences, *A Golden Anniversary* (1945); *The Road Is Yours*, by Reginald M. Cleveland and S. T. Williamson (Greystone Press, 1951); and Larry Freeman's *The Merry Old Mobiles* (Century House, Watkins Glen, N.Y., 1949).

The best book on the design and installation of the Model-T production pattern is *Ford Methods and Ford Shops* (Engineering Magazine Co., 1915), by Horace L. Arnold and Fay L. Faurote. This book is considered a classic by all Ford students. The fact that the authors were completely dominated by the Ford-can-do-no-wrong prejudice does not damage its value as an accurate description of techniques written for the most part in non-technical language. Also useful is the article "Mass Production" signed by Henry Ford in the *Encyclopædia Britannica* (14th ed. *et seq.*) despite its astonishing statement that the "earliest notable appearance" of mass production "falls within the first decade of the twentieth century." Such disregard of history was, of course, famously characteristic.

The personal sketches of Knudsen and Sorensen in Christy Borth's *Masters of Mass Production* (Bobbs-Merrill, 1945) have been helpful. Books on special phases are Louis P. Lochner's on the Peace Ship venture, *Henry Ford—America's Don Quixote* (International Publishers, 1925); Henry Ford Hospital *Collected Papers, 1915–1925;* William Bushnell Stout's autobiography, *So Away I Went* (Bobbs-Merrill, 1951), part of which deals with Ford's aviation activities; Herman Bernstein's *The Truth About the "Protocols of Zion"* (Covici, Friede, 1935) and John Spargo's *The Jew and American Ideals* (Harper, 1921), both dealing with the anti-Semitism of the *Dearborn Independent*; and a number of works that tell of the labor relations of the Ford Motor Company, notably Mary Heaton Vorse's *Labor's New Millions* (Modern Age, 1938) and *The U.A.W. and Walter Reuther,* by Irving Howe and B. J. Widick (Random House, 1949). There is some anecdotal material on Ford's childhood and first jobs in *I Remember Detroit,* by John C. Lodge in collaboration with Milo M. Quaife (Wayne University Press, 1949), and George W. Stark's *In Old Detroit* (Arnold-Powers, 1939).

The author's research in the preparation of his earlier volumes, *Engines of Democracy* (Scribner's, 1940) and *Backgrounds of Power* (Scribner's, 1949), has been helpful in the passages on the philosophy of mass production.

There seems to be no end to the Fordiana in magazines and newspapers over the past fifty years. Much of this material is ephemeral and confusing, published with political, economic, or social axes to grind. The Archives have accumulated about eight hundred magazine pieces reflecting every shade of opinion from reverent worship to apoplectic diatribe. Here and there we find a thoughtful and well-balanced article that has survived the test of time.

Among the most useful to the present study were "The 'Appalling Simplicity' of Henry Ford," in *Current Opinion*, November 1916; "The Case Against Henry Ford" (an ironic title), by Murray Goodwin, in the *American Mercury*, July 1931; "Mr. Ford Doesn't Care," in *Fortune*, December 1933; "Sorensen of the Rouge," in *Fortune*, April 1942; "The Rebirth of Ford," in *Fortune*, May 1947; "Henry Ford II Speaks Out," in the *Atlantic*, December 1947; a "picture-story" in *Life*, August 17, 1942; a number of pieces from *Time* through the 1930's and 1940's cited in the text; Edmund Wilson's "The Despot of Dearborn," in *Scribner's Magazine*, July 1931; and the important series on the Ford collections at Dearborn by Henry A. Haigh and H. M. Cordell in *Michigan History Magazine*, 1925-7.

There is an abundance of primary source material on the Ford Motor Company and on early automotive history in general in *Horseless Age* during the early 1900's. Advertisements, illustrations, reports on automobile shows and on progress in the celebrated Selden case are essential to any Ford study. A few hours spent with the files of this pioneer magazine and the somewhat later *Motor Age* will serve to dissipate many Ford myths and establish certain dates and technical specifications beyond all argument. It is a pity that Mr. Crowther was not more familiar with these simple checking devices!

The most reliable reports of the *Chicago Tribune* libel suit are in the *New York Times* during June and July 1919. Ford's original statement, "History is more or less bunk," was made to Charles M. Wheeler and was published by him in an article in the *Chicago Tribune* on May 25, 1916. It was amplified in an interview with John Reed, reported in *Current Opinion*, November 1916. The original remark was quoted in the *New York Times*, May 20, 1919, and in the trial, Ford *v. Tribune*, July 21, 1919. It has been misquoted ever since.

The *Times* is also a good source on the five-dollar day, January 1914; the Peace Ship, October and November 1915; on Ford's political adventures, May 24, June 11 and 25, 1922; and on his settlement of the Jewish controversy, June 8, 9, 17, 1927.

The primary source on the Dodge suit is John F. Dodge and Horace E. Dodge *v.* Ford Motor Co., State of Michigan Supreme Court, 1918, from which quotation has been made in Chapter Six.

The best thing ever written about the famous car was an essay in *The New Yorker*, reprinted in a thirty-two page book by Putnam in 1936. This magnificent piece of comedy—with tragic overtones—was entitled "Farewell to Model T"; it was written by Lee Strout White and illustrated by Alain.

Publications of the Ford Motor Company that have provided information are a picture book, *Ford at Fifty*, 1953, and an exceedingly useful little booklet called *The Ford Dealer Story*. The latter was published as the fiftieth-anniversary issue of the *Ford Dealer Magazine*, May-June 1953. One of the brief chapters is by the historian Allan Nevins.

These are the principal published sources that have been used in the preparation of this book. In addition, the author has had personal conversations with individuals acquainted with the Fords and with the company. He has also obtained much valuable information from the transcripts of tape recordings of oral reminiscences by all kinds of people—executives, workers, friends of the family, elderly citizens of Detroit, and others—which have been made at the Ford Archives under the able supervision of Mr. Owen Bombard. Visits to the Rouge plant and to the Dearborn museum and Greenfield Village were, of course, essential.

The life of Ford is still a continued story. Perhaps it will be another fifty years before all the material is assembled and a "definitive" biography can be written. A few mysteries may never be solved. There is, however, excellent equipment for the work.

INDEX